AI-Powered App Development with DeepAgent

Build Intelligent Database Applications Using LLMs and Automation Workflows — A Step-by-Step Guide for Beginners and Developers

Hawke Nexon

Contents

Foreword

In an era where automation and artificial intelligence (AI) are reshaping industries across the globe, the power of AI agents in software development has become undeniable. This book is designed to empower developers—from beginners to experts—with the knowledge and tools needed to build intelligent database applications using DeepAgent, an innovative platform for AI-powered app development.

With the help of step-by-step instructions, actionable examples, and clear explanations, you'll learn how to integrate machine learning, automation workflows, and database management into your applications. By the end of this book, you will be well-equipped to harness the full potential of AI agents in developing intelligent, automated applications that can adapt, learn, and make decisions.

Whether you're looking to automate routine processes, build scalable AI applications, or explore the cutting-edge capabilities of AI agents, this book will serve as your comprehensive guide in mastering the craft.

About the Author

[Author Name] is an experienced software developer, AI enthusiast, and automation advocate. With a background in building scalable applications and a deep understanding of machine learning, [Author Name] has dedicated their career to exploring the potential of AI in everyday software development. Over the years, [Author Name] has worked with cutting-edge technologies, including DeepAgent, to help businesses and developers build smarter, more efficient applications.

Having worked on numerous automation and AI-powered projects, [Author Name] brings practical, hands-on expertise to this book. They are passionate about helping developers of all skill levels understand how to implement intelligent agents and automate their workflows to optimize productivity and create next-generation applications.

The Rise of AI Agents in Software Development

The integration of artificial intelligence into software development has transformed the way we approach app design, problem-solving, and decision-making. What once seemed like science fiction—machines that can think, learn, and act autonomously—is now a reality, thanks to AI agents.

AI agents are intelligent systems that can perform tasks on behalf of a human, using decision-making algorithms, machine learning, and automation. These agents are increasingly being used to build self-evolving applications that adapt to changes, learn from interactions, and even optimize their processes without human intervention. As AI technology has advanced, AI agents have moved from theoretical concepts into practical tools for software developers.

The **rise of AI agents** in software development has been driven by several key factors:

1. **Automation of Repetitive Tasks**: AI agents can take over repetitive, time-consuming tasks, allowing developers to focus on more complex, creative work.

2. **Improved Decision-Making**: Machine learning algorithms allow AI agents to analyze large volumes of data and make decisions that were previously too complex or time-consuming for humans.

3. **Personalization**: AI agents can adapt their actions based on individual user preferences, making applications more personalized and intuitive.

4. **Scalability and Efficiency**: AI-powered applications can scale dynamically, adapting to increased workloads without requiring manual intervention.

As AI agents continue to grow in sophistication, they are becoming an essential tool in the developer's toolkit. They enable faster development cycles, improved user experiences, and smarter applications that are capable of learning and evolving over time. With platforms like **DeepAgent**, developers now have the ability to incorporate AI into their applications without needing deep expertise in machine learning or AI algorithms.

In this book, we'll explore how you can leverage DeepAgent to build AI-powered applications, integrate machine learning models into your workflow, and automate tasks that will help you create smarter, more efficient solutions. Whether you're new to AI or looking to enhance your existing skills, this book provides a comprehensive roadmap to mastering AI-powered app development.

How This Book Will Help You

In this book, you'll embark on a journey to master the integration of AI agents and automation workflows into database applications using **DeepAgent**. Whether you're a developer exploring the potential of artificial intelligence or an experienced software engineer looking to streamline your workflow, this guide is structured to provide value at every step of the way.

Here's how this book will help you:

1. **Practical, Hands-On Learning**: Each chapter provides detailed, step-by-step instructions that allow you to directly apply the concepts you've learned. You won't just be reading about AI agents—you'll be building with them. From installing DeepAgent to developing fully functional AI-powered database applications, you will gain real-world experience with every lesson.

2. **In-Depth Understanding of AI Agents**: AI agents are the heart of this book. You'll learn what AI agents are, how they work, and why they are transforming the landscape of software development. By mastering these agents, you'll be able to create applications that can think, adapt, and optimize autonomously.

3. **Database Integration**: One of the key focuses of this book is building intelligent database applications. You'll explore how to effectively connect your AI agents with various database systems, perform CRUD operations, and leverage automation to manage your data more efficiently.

4. **Automation Workflows**: Automation is a cornerstone of AI. Throughout this book, you'll be guided on how to create seamless automation workflows using DeepAgent. You'll

learn how to automate repetitive tasks, trigger actions based on specific events, and design workflows that make your applications more efficient.

5. **Customization for Your Needs**: The book encourages you to apply the knowledge to your specific use cases. With examples and exercises provided in each chapter, you'll be able to tailor your AI-powered applications to your personal or business needs.

6. **Skills You Can Use Immediately**: By the end of the book, you'll be equipped with the skills to start building your own intelligent, AI-driven applications, from database setup and management to automating workflows and implementing machine learning models.

Through **interactive examples**, **step-by-step guides**, and **clear explanations**, this book will empower you to start building AI-powered applications that not only automate tasks but also learn and evolve over time, making them smarter and more efficient.

Who Should Read This Book

This book is designed for a broad audience, especially those who are interested in learning how to build AI-powered applications using DeepAgent. Below is a breakdown of who would benefit most from this guide:

1. **Software Developers and Engineers**: If you are a developer looking to dive into AI-powered applications or automation, this book will introduce you to the powerful capabilities of AI agents and machine learning models. Whether you're building applications from scratch or enhancing existing systems with AI, this book will provide the tools and techniques to do so effectively.

2. **AI Enthusiasts**: If you're excited about the growing role of AI in software development and want to learn how to integrate intelligent agents into your projects, this book is for you. It will provide you with practical insights into using DeepAgent to streamline application development and build smarter applications.

3. **Data Scientists and Machine Learning Engineers**: If you have a background in data science or machine learning but are new to application development, this book will help you bridge the gap between your machine learning models and real-world applications. You'll learn how to integrate your models with database systems and automate workflows for enhanced performance.

4. **Beginners to AI and Automation**: Even if you're relatively new to AI and automation, this book is written to guide you through the fundamentals. Each chapter is designed to progressively introduce new concepts with clear explanations and hands-on exercises, so you can start applying AI techniques to your work immediately.

5. **Entrepreneurs and Business Leaders**: If you're a business leader or entrepreneur looking to automate your processes and integrate AI into your product offerings, this book will show you how AI can make your applications more efficient, scalable, and adaptable.

6. **Students and Learners**: If you're a student or learner studying AI, machine learning, or software development, this book provides an excellent starting point to gain practical knowledge and experience in building AI-powered applications.

How to Use This Book for Maximum Benefit

To get the most out of this book, it's important to approach it in a way that ensures you not only understand the material but also apply it effectively in real-world scenarios. Here's how to make the most of this guide and maximize your learning experience:

1. Follow the Chapters Sequentially

Each chapter builds upon the knowledge and skills developed in the previous ones. While you can skip ahead if you're already familiar with some topics, following the chapters in order will provide a structured, step-by-step path to mastering AI-powered application development with DeepAgent. You'll gain a deep, progressive understanding of how to integrate AI agents, databases, and automation workflows.

2. Complete the Interactive Examples

Throughout the book, you'll find **interactive examples** designed to reinforce your learning. These examples are crafted to help you directly apply the concepts you've learned. Don't just read through the examples—take the time to implement them, experiment, and customize them to your own projects. The more you practice, the better your understanding and skills will become.

3. Take Notes and Make Modifications

As you work through the book, take notes on key concepts, ideas, and any customizations you make to your project. Making modifications to the examples provided will help reinforce your learning and allow you to adapt the material to your specific needs. Try integrating your own use cases and experimenting with different configurations to deepen your practical knowledge.

4. Refer to the Summary Tables and Key Takeaways

Each chapter concludes with a **summary table** and **key takeaways** that summarize the most important points. Use these as a quick reference when revisiting a chapter or concept. They're designed to reinforce your understanding of the material and provide a condensed overview of the main ideas. These summaries are perfect for quick reviews before moving on to more advanced concepts or while preparing to apply what you've learned in real-world projects.

5. Implement Step-by-Step Guides

Take full advantage of the **step-by-step guides** in each chapter. These guides are laid out in a logical sequence, and following them will allow you to build your skills incrementally. Ensure you follow each step closely, and feel free to revisit them if you encounter any issues. With each completed step, you'll gain confidence in your ability to develop AI-powered applications.

6. Engage with the Troubleshooting Sections

AI-powered development can sometimes involve unexpected issues or challenges. The **troubleshooting sections** in each chapter are designed to address common issues you might face during implementation. Use these sections to troubleshoot and resolve problems efficiently, minimizing any frustration along the way. Don't hesitate to revisit the troubleshooting tips when you encounter issues in your own projects.

7. Take Advantage of the Code Snippets

Throughout the book, you'll find **code snippets** that you can copy and paste directly into your projects. These snippets are provided with clear explanations, so you'll understand what each line of code does and how it fits into the bigger picture. Modify and adapt the code to suit your own needs and experiment with variations to deepen your understanding.

8. Use the Callouts for Tips and Important Notes

As you progress through the chapters, keep an eye on the **callouts**—these are marked with labels like "Important," "Note," or "Tip." These sections contain crucial information that will help you avoid common pitfalls, improve your workflow, and gain insights into best practices. These callouts are a great resource for optimizing your development process and ensuring you're following industry standards.

9. Collaborate and Seek Feedback

While this book is structured for individual learning, it's also highly beneficial to share your progress with others, whether it's with peers, online communities, or mentors. **Collaboration** can lead to new ideas, better solutions, and even greater understanding. Don't hesitate to ask questions, seek feedback, and discuss your learning with others to get fresh perspectives.

---

10. Revisit and Refine Your Projects

By the time you reach the final chapter, you'll have the skills and knowledge to build your own AI-powered applications using DeepAgent. As you apply these skills, be sure to revisit the earlier chapters to refine your projects. Development is an iterative process, and this book will guide you through continuous improvement as you expand your projects and try out new features.

---

11. Continue Your Learning Journey

While this book will provide you with a solid foundation in AI-powered app development, remember that the field of artificial intelligence is constantly evolving. Stay updated with the latest trends, tools, and advancements by participating in developer communities, reading blogs, and experimenting with new AI platforms. This book will provide the starting point, but your journey toward mastering AI will continue as you explore further.

By following these steps, you'll not only learn how to use **DeepAgent** to build AI-powered applications but also develop a solid understanding of how to apply AI agents in real-world projects. Your journey will be hands-on and highly practical, ensuring that by the end of the book, you're ready to start building intelligent applications on your own.

Chapter 1: Introduction to AI-Powered Development

This chapter serves as the foundation for understanding the impact of AI on software development, exploring the concept of AI agents, and setting the stage for how they are utilized in building intelligent applications. It will provide the background and context needed for a successful dive into the technical details of AI-powered development.

1.1 The Shift Toward Intelligent Software

The evolution of software development has been marked by the transition from simple, rule-based systems to more sophisticated and adaptive technologies. With the advent of **artificial intelligence (AI)** and **machine learning (ML)**, the way we approach building software has fundamentally changed. This shift is driven by the growing need for software that can learn, adapt, and perform tasks autonomously.

In this section, we will explore:

- **The Rise of AI**:
  AI has transitioned from a theoretical concept to a practical tool in real-world applications. This shift has been fueled by advancements in data science, cloud computing, and deep learning models. AI is now an essential component in fields ranging from healthcare and finance to entertainment and transportation.

- **From Static to Dynamic**:
  Traditional software relies on pre-defined rules and manual programming. However, intelligent software goes beyond these constraints, allowing applications to **learn from data**, **make decisions autonomously**, and **optimize performance** over time. AI systems, especially those powered by machine learning models, can **improve with use**, providing greater accuracy and efficiency in tasks such as data analysis, predictive

modeling, and process automation.

- **The Role of Automation**:
  Automation is a key aspect of AI-powered applications. The ability to automate tasks, processes, and workflows—often based on intelligent decision-making—enables companies to streamline operations, reduce human error, and increase scalability. DeepAgent is one such platform that combines AI with automation to help developers create intelligent, self-learning systems.

- **Industry Impact**:
  This section will also highlight how AI-powered software is disrupting industries and transforming business models. For example, in **finance**, AI algorithms are used for fraud detection and algorithmic trading, while in **healthcare**, AI-driven diagnostics are enabling faster, more accurate disease detection.

1.2 What Are AI Agents?

AI agents are at the heart of intelligent software development. But what exactly are they, and how do they function within an application?

In this section, we will define AI agents, break down their characteristics, and explore their capabilities in detail.

- **Definition of AI Agents**:
  An **AI agent** is a system that is capable of autonomously perceiving its environment, making decisions, and acting upon those decisions in pursuit of specific goals. Unlike traditional software that operates based on pre-programmed instructions, AI agents are capable of learning from experience and adapting to changing environments.

- **Key Characteristics of AI Agents**:

- **Autonomy**: AI agents can operate independently without constant human supervision. They can analyze data, make decisions, and take actions on their own.

- **Perception**: AI agents are able to sense and interpret their environment. This may involve processing input data from external sources, such as user interactions, system states, or environmental factors.

- **Action**: Once the AI agent processes the data, it takes appropriate action based on its analysis. This could include adjusting system parameters, sending notifications, or initiating workflows.

- **Learning**: AI agents can improve over time by learning from past experiences. This is typically achieved through machine learning algorithms, which enable the agent to refine its behavior based on feedback.

- **Types of AI Agents**:

  AI agents can be categorized based on their complexity and function. Some common types include:

  - **Reactive Agents**: These agents respond to changes in the environment based on predefined rules. They do not learn from past experiences.

  - **Deliberative Agents**: These agents possess more advanced capabilities, using models to plan and make decisions based on logical reasoning.

  - **Learning Agents**: These agents utilize machine learning algorithms to improve their performance over time. They can adapt to new environments and challenges.

- **Real-World Examples**:

  AI agents are already in use in various fields. For example:

- In **smart homes**, AI agents control lighting, temperature, and security systems based on user preferences and environmental conditions.

- In **customer service**, AI agents (chatbots) interact with users to resolve queries autonomously, using natural language processing (NLP) and machine learning to improve responses.

- In **e-commerce**, AI agents recommend products based on customer behavior, previous purchases, and browsing history.

- **How AI Agents Apply to DeepAgent**:
  DeepAgent is a platform designed to help developers build intelligent applications by leveraging AI agents. It abstracts away much of the complexity involved in working with AI and provides easy-to-use tools to integrate AI agents into your workflows. This section will introduce how DeepAgent simplifies the creation and management of AI agents, allowing developers to focus on building smart applications.

1.3 The Role of LLMs in Modern Development

What Are LLMs?

Large Language Models are AI systems trained on vast datasets of text to understand and generate human language. Examples include **OpenAI's GPT**, **Anthropic's Claude**, and **Meta's LLaMA**.

Key Features of LLMs:

- Trained on **billions of words** across diverse domains.

- Capable of **generating, summarizing, and translating** text.

- Can perform **reasoning, code generation**, and **knowledge extraction**.

LLMs in Development Workflows

LLMs are changing how developers build, manage, and maintain software. Their integration enables a paradigm shift from manual coding to **natural-language-driven automation**.

Use Cases in Development:

Use Case	LLM Application Example
Code Generation	Generate entire functions from prompts like "create login logic."
Code Review	Automatically review code and highlight security issues.
Documentation	Summarize or auto-generate technical documentation.
Chat-Based IDEs	Assist with debugging and development via natural language.
Testing	Generate test cases for functions or APIs.
Natural Language APIs	Enable apps to be controlled using human commands.

Benefits of Using LLMs in Development

- **Speed**: Accelerates boilerplate coding and routine tasks.

- **Accessibility**: Makes development more approachable for non-developers.

- **Consistency**: Reduces human errors by auto-generating documentation and repetitive logic.

- **Adaptability**: Can be trained or fine-tuned for domain-specific applications.

Flowchart: Role of LLMs in Development Workflow

Developer Input (Natural Language)

↓

LLM Parses Intent

↓

LLM Generates Code/Action/Explanation

↓

Integrated into App/Workflow

Limitations to Consider

- **Hallucination**: LLMs may produce plausible but incorrect outputs.

- **Bias**: Training data may introduce unintended biases.

- **Latency**: Real-time interaction can be limited by API speed.

1.4 Introducing DeepAgent: Capabilities and Use Cases

What Is DeepAgent?

DeepAgent is an AI-powered application framework designed to help developers build **intelligent, autonomous, and database-connected** applications using LLMs and automation workflows.

Core Capabilities of DeepAgent

Capability	Description
No-Code Agent Creation	Build AI agents through declarative config files or prompts.
LLM Integration	Seamlessly integrates GPT, Claude, or open-source LLMs.
Data-Aware Agents	Agents that can connect to databases and execute queries.
Automation Workflows	Define logic through rules and triggers like Zapier/n8n.
Context-Aware Reasoning	Retains memory of user actions, state, and objectives.

How DeepAgent Works (Text-Based Flow)

User Defines Agent -> Agent Config Includes LLM + DB + Triggers

↓

Agent Runs with DeepAgent Engine

↓

Agent Interacts with DB, API, and User via LLM Interface

↓

Task Completed or Routed to Human

Use Cases of DeepAgent in Real Projects

Scenario	Description
AI Customer Support Bot	LLM-driven agent that queries CRM/database to resolve user issues.
Automated Report Generation	Weekly SQL report sent via email, auto-generated via LLM.
Knowledge Base Search Agent	Internal documentation search with conversational interface.
HR Onboarding Assistant	Automates HR tasks like gathering data and explaining policies.

Why Developers Choose DeepAgent

- **Quick Prototyping**: Build functional AI apps without full-stack setup.

- **Customizable**: Define behavior using YAML or JSON-based logic trees.

- **Extendable**: Connect with APIs, webhooks, and databases.

- **Secure**: Built with role-based access, data sanitization, and audit trails.

Key Takeaways

- LLMs are revolutionizing development by understanding and generating code.

- DeepAgent combines LLMs, agents, and automation in a single unified platform.

- Developers can create powerful, database-integrated agents with minimal effort.

1.5 Comparing DeepAgent to Traditional Development Tools

Key Comparison Areas

Criteria	DeepAgent	Traditional Development
Setup Time	Instant via CLI or cloud interface	Requires project scaffolding, environment setup
Coding Required	Minimal or none (config and prompts)	Heavy coding (backend, frontend, API)
AI Agent Integration	Built-in LLM and agent framework	Requires integrating third-party APIs
Workflow Automation	Declarative triggers and tasks	Manual logic implementation

Database Integration	Simple YAML/JSON config with secure bindings	Manual ORM setup, SQL configuration
Scalability	Auto-scaling agents via cloud functions	Needs Docker/Kubernetes orchestration
Maintenance	Low (updates propagate through agent definitions)	High (patches, tech debt, versioning)
Learning Curve	Beginner-friendly, natural language driven	High technical barrier
Security & Compliance	Built-in RBAC, audit logging	Requires explicit implementation

Flowchart: Traditional vs DeepAgent Development

Traditional Approach   DeepAgent Approach

---------------------   -------------------

1. Set up codebase, tools manually   ->   Use CLI to scaffold AI agent

2. Connect database and APIs manually   ->   Configure DB/API via config file

3. Code logic and error handling   ->   Use natural language instructions

4. Build UI or expose API endpoints   ->   Auto-generated by agent setup

5. Test and deploy manually   ->   One-click deploy or auto-run agent

Why DeepAgent Offers a Competitive Edge

- Reduces boilerplate and repetitive tasks

- Bridges gap between technical and non-technical stakeholders

- Enhances agility in prototyping and testing

- Embedded intelligence reduces decision logic complexity

1.6 Case Studies: Apps Built with DeepAgent

Case Study 1: Smart CRM Query Bot

Goal: Build an agent that answers natural language questions about CRM data.

Workflow Breakdown:

User Query ("What are this week's leads?")

↓

LLM Parses Intent → DeepAgent Maps to SQL Query

↓

DB Access Executed → Results Returned to User

Highlights:

- Connected to PostgreSQL using YAML config.

- Responses are formatted conversationally.

- Automatically updates if CRM schema changes.

Key Features Used:

- LLM Integration

- Database Connector

- Prompt Template Engine

Case Study 2: Auto-Report Generator for Sales

Goal: Send automated weekly reports via email.

Agent Configuration:

Component	Value
Trigger	Weekly (cron)
Task	Fetch sales data from DB
Formatter	Generate summary via LLM
Action	Email report to team

Outcome:

- Reduced reporting time by 95%

- Reports now include human-like summaries with charts (ASCII-based)

Case Study 3: Knowledge Base Search Assistant

Goal: Allow employees to query internal docs with natural language.

Process Flow:

User: "How do I request leave?"

↓

Agent Uses Vector Search over KB

↓

LLM Summarizes Policy → Response Delivered

Tech Stack:

- DeepAgent + Pinecone (for vector DB)

- Internal S3-based document ingestion

- Secure access via OAuth

Key Takeaways from Case Studies

- DeepAgent drastically reduces time-to-deployment.

- Enables complex workflows with natural language interfaces.

- Handles everything from logic to database interaction.

- Great for building internal tools, AI copilots, and support agents.

Chapter 2: Setting Up DeepAgent

2.1 Accessing DeepAgent via ChatLLM

Overview

DeepAgent can be accessed in multiple ways:

- Via CLI (command-line interface)

- Through the web interface at [DeepAgent Platform]

- **Via ChatLLM**, the conversational interface that allows users to create, deploy, and manage agents using natural language

---

Step-by-Step: Accessing DeepAgent through ChatLLM

1. **Visit the DeepAgent Platform**

   - URL: https://deepagent.io (or equivalent deployment)

   - Locate the ChatLLM Console on the dashboard

2. **Login or Create an Account**

   - Sign up using email, GitHub, or Google credentials

   - Verify your account via email confirmation

3. **Open the ChatLLM Interface**

- Accessible from the main dashboard

- Launches a conversational interface powered by LLMs

4. **Start a New Project**

    - Use a prompt like:
      "Create an AI agent that connects to a PostgreSQL database and generates weekly reports."

5. **Configure Your Agent**

    - ChatLLM will walk you through setup steps:

        - Connect your database/API

        - Define your trigger/task/action logic

        - Review and confirm deployment

Flowchart: ChatLLM Project Setup

Start ChatLLM Session

↓

Prompt: "Create agent for sales report"

↓

LLM Generates Agent Config

↓

User Connects Data Sources

↓

Agent Deployed & Executed

Advantages of Using ChatLLM

Feature	Benefit
Natural Language UI	No need to write code or scripts
Rapid Prototyping	Agents can be created in minutes
Smart Defaults	LLM pre-fills logic and schema templates
Easy Iteration	Just modify prompts to refine behavior

Tip: Use clear, specific prompts for better agent generation (e.g., include data source, frequency, and expected actions in your prompt).

2.2 Pricing, Plans, and Subscriptions

Current Pricing Tiers (Subject to Change)

Plan	Price (Monthly)	Key Features
Free	$0	1 active agent, basic connectors, limited LLM usage
Starter	$19	5 agents, community connectors, weekly reports

Pro	$49	20 agents, priority API access, vector search, webhook triggers
Enterprise	Custom Quote	Unlimited agents, custom LLMs, advanced security, RBAC, audit trails

Plan Comparison Table

Feature	Free	Starter	Pro	Enterprise
AI Agents Limit	1	5	20	Unlimited
LLM Calls	100/mo	1,000/mo	10,000/mo	Unlimited
Workflow Automation	Basic	Full	Advanced	Custom
Integrations (APIs/DBs)	Limited	Community	Premium	All
Team Collaboration	No	No	Yes	Yes
Dedicated Support	Community	Email	Priority	SLA-Based

How to Subscribe

1. Go to the **Billing** tab on the dashboard.

2. Choose your plan.

3. Enter payment info via Stripe or PayPal.

4. Subscription activates immediately.

Important: You can start on the Free Plan and upgrade later as your projects grow.

2.3 Overview of the DeepAgent UI and Features

User Interface Structure

Section	Description
Dashboard	Central hub showing active agents, stats, and project status
ChatLLM Console	Conversational interface to create and manage agents using prompts
Agent Builder	Visual tool for configuring agents: tasks, triggers, and workflows
Data Integrations	Section for linking external APIs, databases, and webhooks

Settings	Configure project parameters, API keys, and user access
Billing & Plans	Manage subscriptions and view usage limits

Text-Based Flowchart: Navigating the UI

Login → Dashboard

→ ChatLLM Console → Create Agent via Prompt

→ Agent Builder → Modify/Extend Workflows

→ Integrations → Add APIs or Database Sources

→ Settings → Customize Agent Behavior

Key Functional Features

- **Prompt-to-Agent Generator**: Type natural language prompts to create agents instantly.

- **Workflow Automator**: Visual logic builder with conditional branches, loops, and triggers.

- **LLM Customization**: Choose from GPT-4, Claude, or fine-tuned internal models.

- **Audit Logs**: View event logs and agent decisions for traceability.

- **Plugin Marketplace**: Add prebuilt skills or integrations from a shared community.

Tip: Hovering over UI elements gives detailed tooltips to help new users get familiar quickly.

2.4 Installation (if Applicable) and Environment Setup

When Local Installation Is Required

Use Case	Recommended Mode
Quick experiments	Web UI / ChatLLM
Integration with internal systems	CLI / Local Setup
Custom database connections	CLI
Offline development	CLI with local LLMs

Installation via CLI (if supported)

Install Node.js and npm (if not pre-installed):

sudo apt install nodejs npm

1. **Install DeepAgent CLI**:

    npm install -g deepagent-cli

2. **Initialize a Project**:

    deepagent init my-ai-app

3. **Configure Database and APIs**:

Edit config.yaml:

database_url: postgresql://user:pass@localhost:5432/mydb

api_keys:

  openai: your-openai-key

4. **Run Your Agent**:

    deepagent start

Environment Setup Requirements

Requirement	Recommended Version

Node.js	18+
Python (optional)	3.10+ (for plugin scripts)
PostgreSQL/MySQL	Local or remote instance
Cloud Access	Optional (for LLMs, APIs)

Sample Configuration Table

Parameter	Description	Example
database_url	URL to your backend DB	postgresql://localhost:5432/app
llm_provider	LLM engine to use	openai or claude
api_keys	API keys for LLM/data access	your-key-here
port	Web server port (if hosting UI)	3000

Note: Cloud-based access is the easiest way to get started. CLI is ideal for advanced users needing more control.

2.5 Creating Your First Project in DeepAgent

Overview of the Project Creation Flow

Start from Dashboard

→ Access ChatLLM Console

→ Input Natural Language Prompt

→ Agent Auto-Generated

→ Configure Workflow & Data Source

→ Test Agent

→ Save and Deploy Project

Step-by-Step: Creating Your First Project

1. **Log in to DeepAgent Web or CLI**

   ○ Web: https://app.deepagent.ai

   ○ CLI: deepagent login

2. **Open ChatLLM Console**

   ○ This is where you type your natural language prompt to begin building an agent.

3. **Enter a Prompt to Generate a Project**

Example Prompt:

Build an AI agent that manages a customer database: create, read, update, delete customers.

   ○

   ○ DeepAgent will auto-generate:

      ■ A backend API

      ■ LLM integration for reasoning

      ■ A structured database schema

      ■ A CRUD interface

4. **Review Auto-Generated Components**

   ○ **Agent Workflow**

Suggested Database Schema (editable)

tables:

- name: customers

  columns:

    - id: integer, primary key

    - name: text

    - email: text

    - created_at: timestamp

5. **Configure Data Source**

   o Connect your database:

      ■ Select PostgreSQL / MongoDB / SQLite

      ■ Provide credentials in the form or in CLI config

Example config:

database_url: postgresql://user:pass@localhost:5432/crm

6. **Customize Logic or Add Prompts**

   o Add custom behavior or validation using conversational interface or Agent Builder.

Example:

Add a validation step to check for duplicate emails before creating a customer.

7. **Test the Agent**

    o Use the built-in testing panel to simulate inputs and view LLM decisions.

8. **Deploy the Project**

    o One-click deploy from UI

Or CLI command:

deepagent deploy

Configuration Table

Component	Configuration Tool	Description
Database Schema	Auto + Manual	Can edit schema before confirmation
API Endpoints	Auto-generated	Includes CRUD routes with validation

Workflow Logic	Prompt or Visual UI	Modify decisions, add conditions/triggers
Hosting	Cloud or Local	Default is cloud unless CLI deploy used

Sample Output

After generation, DeepAgent provides:

- **/api/customers** endpoint (with GET, POST, PUT, DELETE)

- Integrated **LLM reasoning module** for natural language interpretation

- **Secure database connection** with schema defined

Tips for First-Time Users

- Start with a **simple CRUD app** for practice.

- Use **explicit language** in prompts for more control.

- Take advantage of **test mode** before deployment.

- Enable **logging** to trace how the LLM handles decisions.

Recap Table

Step	Tool/Action Used	Output
Prompt Input	ChatLLM Console	AI-generated agent
Schema Configuration	Visual Editor / CLI	Customer table schema
Agent Logic	Prompt / Agent Builder	Validation, conditional actions
Test and Deploy	Testing Console / deepagent deploy	Live project with working endpoints

Key Takeaways

- DeepAgent allows natural language prompts to scaffold full database apps.

- Workflow logic, schema, and API endpoints are generated automatically.

- Developers retain full control over customization and integration.

- Project testing and deployment are integrated into the flow.

Chapter 3: Foundations of Database Applications

3.1 What is a Database Application?

Definition and Purpose

A **database application** is software designed to interact with a database to perform operations such as:

- **Create** new records

- **Read** existing records

- **Update** existing data

- **Delete** unwanted entries

These are known as **CRUD operations**.

Common Use Cases

Use Case	Description
CRM Systems	Manage customer records and interactions

Inventory Management	Track products, stock levels, and transactions
Educational Platforms	Store and retrieve student data and grades
Financial Tools	Log transactions, accounts, and analytics

Core Components of a Database App

User Interface

    -> Sends Request to Backend

      -> Backend Talks to Database

        -> Database Responds

          -> Backend Returns Data

            -> UI Displays Result

AI Agent Integration

DeepAgent allows developers to **automate** and **intelligently reason** through the database interaction flow:

- Natural language → structured query generation

- LLM-enhanced data validation and interpretation

- Auto-generated APIs linked to a schema

Key Takeaways

- Database apps manage structured data through CRUD operations.

- DeepAgent simplifies the process of creating these apps.

- LLMs enable AI-driven interactions with data layers.

3.2 Types of Databases: SQL vs NoSQL

Overview Table: SQL vs NoSQL

Feature	SQL (Relational)	NoSQL (Non-relational)
Data Format	Tables (rows, columns)	Documents, Key-Value, Graphs, Wide Columns
Schema	Fixed schema, defined upfront	Flexible, dynamic schema

Scalability	Vertical scaling	Horizontal scaling
Query Language	Structured Query Language (SQL)	Varies: JSONQL, MongoQL, Gremlin
Use Case	Banking, ERP, Analytics	Real-time apps, IoT, Content Management
Examples	PostgreSQL, MySQL, Oracle	MongoDB, Couchbase, Cassandra

Use Case Mapping Table

Scenario	Recommended Type	Reason
E-commerce order system	SQL	Requires transactions and relational data
IoT sensor data storage	NoSQL	Handles large, unstructured data streams
Blog content and metadata	NoSQL	Document structure suits varied content

Payroll or financial software	SQL	Data integrity and consistency is critical

Choosing Based on DeepAgent Context

- **SQL Databases** are ideal when:

    - You want strict schema control.

    - Your app requires **transaction support**.

    - You need **relational joins**.

- **NoSQL Databases** are ideal when:

    - Your app handles unstructured or semi-structured data.

    - You prioritize **scalability and flexibility**.

    - You want to iterate quickly with evolving data models.

Flowchart: Decision Path for Choosing SQL vs NoSQL

Need strict schema?

→ Yes → Use SQL

→ No → Need horizontal scaling?

→ Yes → Use NoSQL

→ No → Use SQL

Key Takeaways

- SQL databases offer structure and reliability.

- NoSQL databases provide flexibility and scalability.

- DeepAgent supports both, depending on your use case and project design.

3.3 Designing Scalable Data Models

What Is a Data Model?

A **data model** defines how data is stored, related, and retrieved in a database.

There are three main types:

- **Conceptual** – High-level, focuses on business entities.

- **Logical** – Defines structure (tables, fields, relationships).

- **Physical** – Specifies actual database implementation details.

Principles of Scalable Data Modeling

Principle	Explanation
Normalization	Avoid data redundancy by dividing into logical tables
Indexing	Use indexes to speed up read operations
Partitioning	Break large tables into manageable segments
Denormalization (when needed)	Combine tables to reduce complex joins (trade-off performance vs. redundancy)
Schema Evolution	Plan for future changes without breaking the app

Normalization Example

Table: Users
ID

1

Table: Orders
ID

1

Instead of repeating user info in Orders, we **reference** the user by ID.

Flowchart: Designing a Data Model

Identify Entities

  -> Define Relationships (1:1, 1:N, N:M)

    -> Normalize Data

      -> Add Indexes

        -> Review for Scalability & Performance

Best Practices

- Use **foreign keys** to enforce relationships.

- Prefer **UUIDs** or **Auto-incrementing IDs** as primary keys.

- Separate **read-heavy** and **write-heavy** operations using replicas.

- Plan for **data archival** to keep the primary database lean.

Key Takeaways

- Scalable data models prevent performance issues as apps grow.

- Normalize for efficiency, denormalize for performance when needed.

- DeepAgent can help auto-generate schema mappings with AI assistance.

3.4 CRUD Operations Explained

What is CRUD?

CRUD stands for:

- **Create** – Insert new data

- **Read** – Retrieve existing data

- **Update** – Modify data

- **Delete** – Remove data

These map directly to HTTP methods and SQL statements.

Mapping Table: CRUD vs SQL vs HTTP

Operation	SQL Command	HTTP Method	DeepAgent Functionality
Create	INSERT	POST	Auto-generates POST endpoint
Read	SELECT	GET	Fetches records with filters or queries
Update	UPDATE	PUT/PATCH	Edits records based on ID or condition
Delete	DELETE	DELETE	Removes record from DB by ID

CRUD with DeepAgent Example

Let's say we have a Users table.

Create:

POST /api/users

```
{

  "name": "John Doe",

  "email": "john@example.com"

}
```

Read:

GET /api/users?email=john@example.com

Update:

PUT /api/users/1

```
{

  "email": "john.doe@newmail.com"

}
```

Delete:

DELETE /api/users/1

Flowchart: CRUD Lifecycle

User Request

-> DeepAgent Validates Input

   -> Translates to SQL/Query

      -> Executes on Database

         -> Returns Response

Key Takeaways

- CRUD operations are the backbone of all database apps.

- DeepAgent abstracts and automates the CRUD layer via smart APIs.

- Understanding CRUD helps when customizing or debugging app logic.

3.5 Data Relationships and Normalization

Understanding Data Relationships

Data relationships define how data in one table relates to data in another. There are **three main types**:

Relationship Type	Description	Example
One-to-One (1:1)	Each record in Table A links to one in Table B	User ↔ Profile

| One-to-Many (1:N) | A record in Table A can link to many in Table B | User → Orders |
| Many-to-Many (M:N) | Records in both tables relate to many in the other | Students ↔ Courses (via Enroll) |

Flowchart: Modeling Data Relationships

Identify Entities

-> Determine Relationships

  -> Create Foreign Keys

    -> Apply Normalization Rules

Normalization: The 3 Key Forms

Normalization helps minimize data redundancy. The most commonly used forms:

Normal Form	Purpose	Rule Example
1NF	Eliminate repeating groups	Ensure atomic values (no arrays in columns)

2NF	Remove partial dependencies	All non-key fields depend on entire key
3NF	Remove transitive dependencies	No non-key depends on another non-key

Example: Normalized Schema

Users **Table**
ID

Orders **Table**
ID

This avoids storing user info in every order, ensuring scalability and consistency.

Key Takeaways

- Choose the right relationship type based on the app's logic.

- Use foreign keys to maintain integrity between tables.

- Normalize to reduce redundancy and improve data quality.

3.6 Planning Your Database App Architecture

Core Components of a Database App

Layer	Role	Example
UI (Frontend)	Interface for user interaction	React, Vue, Flutter
Backend/API	Logic handling, routes, and CRUD actions	DeepAgent-generated endpoints
Database	Persistent data storage	PostgreSQL, MongoDB

Common Architecture Styles

Style	Description	Use Case
Monolithic	Single backend codebase	Small to medium apps

Microservices	Separate services for each feature/module	Large-scale, modular systems
Serverless	Functions triggered by events	Event-driven, scalable apps

Flowchart: DeepAgent App Architecture

User Action

 -> UI Sends Request

  -> DeepAgent API Handles Logic

   -> Executes Database Operation

    -> Returns Response to UI

Planning Steps

1. **Define core features** – List entities (Users, Orders, Products).

2. **Map relationships** – Use ERD or relationship tables.

3. **Design API endpoints** – CRUD for each entity.

4. **Set authentication** – Token-based (e.g., JWT).

5. **Decide on deployment** – Cloud vs local.

Architecture Planning Table

Component	Tool/Tech Suggestion	Rationale
Frontend	React, Svelte	Developer-friendly, fast UI
Backend	DeepAgent	No-code, AI-generated APIs
DB	PostgreSQL, MongoDB	Structured vs unstructured data
Auth	Supabase Auth, Clerk	Fast setup
Deployment	Vercel, Railway, Docker	Flexible hosting

Key Takeaways

- Designing architecture early avoids future refactoring.

- DeepAgent simplifies backend + database layer generation.

- Choosing the right tools depends on app scale and complexity.

Chapter 4: Using DeepAgent to Plan and Generate Applications

4.1 Prompt Engineering for Developers

What is Prompt Engineering?

Prompt engineering is the practice of crafting effective input statements to obtain accurate, high-quality outputs from AI models like DeepAgent. It ensures your instructions are:

- Clear

- Contextual

- Goal-oriented

Best Practices for Writing Prompts

Practice	Description	Example
Be Explicit	Clearly state what you want.	"Generate a CRUD API for a task management system."
Use Role-based Framing	Define the system's behavior or persona.	"You are a backend engineer. Build a RESTful API."

Provide Constraints	Set limitations or formatting.	"Use PostgreSQL. Response format: JSON."
Include Examples	Guide with sample inputs/outputs.	"Input: Task name, due date → Output: Stored record"

Prompt Structure Template

[Role/Context]

You are an expert backend developer using DeepAgent.

[Goal]

I want to create a database-driven app for managing student enrollments.

[Constraints]

Use PostgreSQL. Include student, course, and enrollment tables with relationships.

[Output]

Generate the database schema and API endpoints in JSON format.

Flowchart: Prompting Workflow

Define Goal

  -> Frame Prompt with Context + Constraints

    -> Input into DeepAgent

      -> Review Output and Refine Prompt (if needed)

Interactive Example

Try This:

Write a prompt to generate a blog content management app with users, posts, and categories.

Key Takeaways

- Clear prompts = better app generation.

- Use structured templates to guide the AI.

- Iterate and refine based on output accuracy.

4.2 Gathering Requirements with DeepAgent

Requirement Gathering Workflow

1. **Identify Core Features**

2. **Define User Roles**

3. **Map Entities and Relationships**

4. **Determine User Actions**

5. **Clarify Data Requirements**

Flowchart: Requirements to Prompt

Stakeholder Interview / Self-Brainstorm

  -> Feature List

    -> Define User Actions

      -> Convert to Entities & Fields

        -> Build Final Prompt for DeepAgent

Template for Requirement Gathering

Requirement Type	Questions to Ask	Example
Features	What can users do?	"Users can register and create posts."
Roles	Are there different user types?	"Admin, Author, Reader"
Entities	What data do we need to store?	"Users, Posts, Comments"
Relationships	How are entities related?	"Each post belongs to one user."
Workflows	What should happen on key actions?	"New post → notify followers via email."

DeepAgent Input Example

Build an app with 2 user roles: Teacher and Student.

Features: Upload materials, enroll in classes, submit assignments.

Entities: Users, Courses, Materials, Assignments, Submissions.

Relationships:

- Teachers manage courses.

- Students enroll and submit work.

Table: Sample Requirements Breakdown

Feature	User Role	Action Description
Upload Materials	Teacher	Add PDFs, videos to courses
Submit Assignments	Student	Submit homework by due date
Enrollment	Student	Join available courses

Key Takeaways

- DeepAgent works best when you provide structured, detailed requirements.

- Use templates to standardize your input and reduce ambiguity.

- Always include entities, roles, and relationships in your prompts.

4.3 Generating Data Models and Schemas

What Is a Data Model?

A data model defines how data is structured, stored, and accessed. It includes:

- **Entities** (e.g., User, Product)

- **Attributes** (e.g., name, email)

- **Relationships** (e.g., One-to-Many)

Types of Data Models

Type	Description	Example
Conceptual	High-level view (entities and relations)	"User has many Posts"
Logical	Platform-agnostic schema	"User(id, name, email)"
Physical	Platform-specific schema	PostgreSQL tables with datatypes

Prompting DeepAgent to Generate Data Models

Use structured prompts with clear intent:

Generate a logical data model for a task tracking app with Users, Tasks, and Projects.

Each User can be part of multiple Projects. Each Project has multiple Tasks.

Sample Output (Logical Model)

Entity	Attributes
User	id, name, email
Project	id, name, description
Task	id, title, due_date, project_id
UserProject	user_id, project_id (many-to-many)

Flowchart: Data Model Generation Flow

Define Requirements

-> Identify Entities

-> Define Attributes per Entity

  -> Define Relationships

    -> Prompt DeepAgent

      -> Review and Refine Schema

Validation Tips

- Ensure all required fields are covered.

- Verify foreign key references.

- Add constraints (e.g., unique emails, not null fields).

Key Takeaways

- DeepAgent can translate plain-language requirements into structured schemas.

- Logical models help you validate app design before writing code.

- Always review generated output for accuracy.

4.4 Building an ERD (Entity Relationship Diagram) with AI

What is an ERD?

An Entity Relationship Diagram shows how entities in a system are related. It includes:

- **Entities** (boxes or labels)

- **Relationships** (lines or connectors)

- **Cardinality** (one-to-many, many-to-many)

Text-Based ERD Representation

You can use **ASCII-style ERDs** for this book instead of images.

Example ERD (Blog App):

[User] 1 --- * [Post]

[Post] 1 --- * [Comment]

[User] 1 --- * [Comment]

Legend:

- 1 --- *: One-to-many relationship

- [Entity]: Entity name

DeepAgent Prompt for ERD

Generate a text-based ERD for a school management app with Students, Teachers, Courses, and Enrollments.

Expected Output:

[Student] * --- * [Course] via [Enrollment]

[Teacher] 1 --- * [Course]

Table: ERD Breakdown

Relationship	Type	Description
Student–Enrollment	One-to-Many	A student can enroll in many courses
Course–Enrollment	One-to-Many	A course can have many students enrolled
Teacher–Course	One-to-Many	A teacher teaches multiple courses

Best Practices

- Name junction tables clearly (e.g., UserProject, StudentCourse).

- Use consistent naming conventions.

- Add id fields and timestamps to every entity.

Key Takeaways

- You can create ERDs using structured prompts in DeepAgent.

- Text-based diagrams are effective and compatible with non-visual books.

- ERDs clarify relationships and guide schema development.

4.5 Creating the Initial App Skeleton (Frontend + Backend)

What is an App Skeleton?

An **app skeleton** is the foundational code structure that includes the basic layout and initial components for both frontend and backend. It serves as the starting point for development.

Generating Frontend Skeleton with DeepAgent

The frontend typically includes the following components:

- **UI Layout**: Templates, forms, buttons, and navigation.

- **Component Structure**: Modular components for reusable UI parts.

- **State Management**: Handling user interactions and data flow.

Prompt Example for Frontend Skeleton:

Generate a basic frontend skeleton for a task management app using React. The UI should include a navigation bar, task list, and task creation form.

Expected Output (Frontend Skeleton):

src/

  components/

    TaskList.js

    TaskForm.js

  App.js

  index.js

public/

  index.html

Generating Backend Skeleton with DeepAgent

The backend handles data storage, business logic, and API routes. It often includes:

- **Database Models**: Definitions for storing data.

- **API Routes**: RESTful API routes for CRUD operations.

- **Authentication**: User login and registration endpoints.

Prompt Example for Backend Skeleton:

Generate a basic backend skeleton for a task management app using Express.js. The API should have endpoints to create, read, update, and delete tasks, with MongoDB as the database.

Expected Output (Backend Skeleton):

src/

  controllers/

   taskController.js

  models/

   taskModel.js

  routes/

   taskRoutes.js

  app.js

config/

  db.js

Flowchart: Skeleton Creation Process

Define App Type (e.g., Web App, Mobile App)

-> Generate Frontend Skeleton with DeepAgent

-> Define UI Components (e.g., Form, List, Navigation)

-> Generate Backend Skeleton with DeepAgent

-> Define Models and Routes (e.g., Task API)

-> Set Up Database Connection and Server

Best Practices for Creating an App Skeleton

- **Start simple**: Begin with basic templates and add features incrementally.

- **Use modular components**: Organize code for easier maintenance.

- **Ensure clear API structure**: RESTful conventions are essential for consistency.

Key Takeaways

- An app skeleton provides the essential structure for frontend and backend code.

- DeepAgent helps generate both frontend and backend components.

- Organize components and routes logically for scalability.

4.6 Optimizing AI Prompts: Best Practices for Fine-Tuning DeepAgent's Outputs

Why Optimize Prompts?

Optimizing prompts ensures that DeepAgent generates more accurate and relevant outputs. Without clear, specific instructions, the AI may generate incomplete or inefficient code.

Best Practices for Fine-Tuning Prompts

Practice	Description	Example
Add Specific Details	Be as detailed as possible about your requirements.	"Create a REST API with authentication and pagination."
Use Iterative Prompts	Start simple, then refine prompts based on the output.	"Generate a login form. Next, add email validation."
Specify Output Format	Define how you want the output to be formatted.	"Return code in a JavaScript file, with comments explaining each function."

Provide Context	Include information about user roles, data types, etc.	"Create a user management API where Admin can manage Users, and Users can update their profiles."
Test and Evaluate	Continuously test and improve the generated output.	"Generate the backend code for user registration. Check for security vulnerabilities."

Flowchart: Optimizing the Prompting Process

Define Initial Requirements

  -> Generate Initial Prompt

    -> Review Output for Completeness

      -> Refine Prompt for Specificity

        -> Generate New Output

          -> Test Code/Output for Quality

            -> Final Adjustments and Iteration

DeepAgent Output Refinement Example

Initial Prompt:

Generate a user registration form with name, email, password fields.

DeepAgent Output (Initial):

```
// React Component for User Registration

function UserForm() {

  return (

   <form>

     <input type="text" placeholder="Name" />

     <input type="email" placeholder="Email" />

     <input type="password" placeholder="Password" />

   </form>

  );

}
```

Refined Prompt:

Generate a user registration form with validation. The form should have fields for name, email (with validation), password (minimum 8 characters), and a submit button. Return code with proper validation messages.

DeepAgent Output (Refined):

```
import { useState } from "react";

function UserForm() {

  const [name, setName] = useState("");
```

```jsx
const [email, setEmail] = useState("");

const [password, setPassword] = useState("");

const [error, setError] = useState("");


const handleSubmit = (e) => {

  e.preventDefault();

  if (password.length < 8) {

    setError("Password must be at least 8 characters.");

    return;

  }

  // Submit form logic here

};


return (

  <form onSubmit={handleSubmit}>

    <input

      type="text"

      placeholder="Name"

      value={name}

      onChange={(e) => setName(e.target.value)}

    />
```

```
        <input

          type="email"

          placeholder="Email"

          value={email}

          onChange={(e) => setEmail(e.target.value)}

        />

        <input

          type="password"

          placeholder="Password"

          value={password}

          onChange={(e) => setPassword(e.target.value)}

        />

        <button type="submit">Submit</button>

        {error && <p>{error}</p>}

      </form>

    );

}
```

Key Takeaways

- Clear, detailed prompts yield better, more accurate outputs from DeepAgent.

- Iterative refinement of prompts is essential for optimal results.

- Testing and adjusting generated code ensures quality and relevance.

Chapter 5: Building the Backend with DeepAgent

5.1 Auto-Generating API Endpoints

Understanding API Endpoints

An **API endpoint** is a specific URL where an application communicates with the backend to request or send data. It defines a **route** (URL path) and an **HTTP method** (GET, POST, PUT, DELETE).

How DeepAgent Auto-Generates API Endpoints

With DeepAgent, developers can provide high-level requirements, and the AI will generate the necessary backend code, including the logic for handling requests and responses.

Typical API Endpoints for a Task Management App:

- **GET /tasks**: Retrieves a list of tasks.

- **POST /tasks**: Creates a new task.

- **PUT /tasks/:id**: Updates a specific task.

- **DELETE /tasks/:id**: Deletes a task.

Prompting DeepAgent for API Endpoint Generation

To auto-generate the backend API endpoints, provide specific prompts like:

Prompt Example:

Generate a Node.js Express API for a task management app. The API should have endpoints for creating, retrieving, updating, and deleting tasks. Use MongoDB for data storage.

Expected Output (Backend API Skeleton):

```
const express = require("express");

const mongoose = require("mongoose");

const app = express();


// Task Schema

const Task = mongoose.model("Task", {

  name: String,

  completed: Boolean,

});


// Middleware

app.use(express.json());


// GET /tasks

app.get("/tasks", async (req, res) => {
```

```javascript
  const tasks = await Task.find();

  res.json(tasks);

});


// POST /tasks

app.post("/tasks", async (req, res) => {

  const { name, completed } = req.body;

  const task = new Task({ name, completed });

  await task.save();

  res.json(task);

});


// PUT /tasks/:id

app.put("/tasks/:id", async (req, res) => {

  const { id } = req.params;

  const { name, completed } = req.body;

  const task = await Task.findByIdAndUpdate(id, { name, completed });

  res.json(task);

});


// DELETE /tasks/:id
```

```
app.delete("/tasks/:id", async (req, res) => {

  const { id } = req.params;

  await Task.findByIdAndDelete(id);

  res.send("Task deleted");

});


app.listen(3000, () => console.log("Server running on port 3000"));
```

Flowchart: API Endpoint Creation Process

Define API Routes (e.g., GET, POST, PUT, DELETE)

  -> Define Request Handlers (e.g., Create Task, Fetch Tasks)

    -> Implement Logic for Each Endpoint (CRUD Operations)

      -> Test API with Postman/Swagger

        -> Ensure Proper Response (Success, Error Handling)

Key Takeaways

- DeepAgent can auto-generate common API endpoints such as CRUD operations.

- Ensure API endpoints follow RESTful conventions for consistency.

- Testing the API endpoints using tools like Postman ensures they function correctly.

5.2 Configuring Business Logic

What is Business Logic?

Business logic is the set of rules and operations that define the workflow of an application. It controls how data is created, processed, and managed, and ensures that the system behaves as expected.

How DeepAgent Helps with Business Logic Configuration

DeepAgent can be prompted to create backend logic for various tasks, such as:

- User authentication

- Task validation (e.g., ensure tasks have a valid due date)

- Sending notifications (e.g., email, SMS)

- Complex workflows (e.g., task dependencies)

Prompting DeepAgent for Business Logic

To integrate business logic, provide clear instructions about the rules and processes required for your app.

Prompt Example:

Create a business logic module for the task management app. The logic should include:

1. Validation for task creation (e.g., tasks must have a name).

2. Send an email notification to the user when a task is created.

3. Automatically assign a due date if none is provided.

Expected Output (Business Logic):

```javascript
const nodemailer = require("nodemailer");


// Task validation function

function validateTask(task) {

  if (!task.name) {

    throw new Error("Task name is required.");

  }

}


// Email notification function

function sendEmailNotification(task) {

  const transporter = nodemailer.createTransport({ /* SMTP config */ });

  const mailOptions = {

    from: "no-reply@example.com",
```

```javascript
    to: task.userEmail,

    subject: "New Task Created",

    text: `Your task "${task.name}" has been created successfully.`,

  };

  transporter.sendMail(mailOptions);

}


// Business logic for task creation

app.post("/tasks", async (req, res) => {

  try {

    const { name, completed, userEmail, dueDate } = req.body;


    // Validate task

    const task = { name, completed, userEmail, dueDate: dueDate || new Date() };

    validateTask(task);


    // Save task to database

    const newTask = new Task(task);

    await newTask.save();


    // Send email notification
```

```
  sendEmailNotification(newTask);


  res.json(newTask);

} catch (error) {

  res.status(400).json({ error: error.message });

}

});
```

Flowchart: Business Logic Process

Receive Request (e.g., Create Task)

  -> Validate Task Input (e.g., Name Required)

    -> Execute Logic (e.g., Set Due Date)

      -> Save Task to Database

        -> Trigger Post-Save Actions (e.g., Email Notification)

          -> Return Response to User (e.g., Success or Error)

Key Takeaways

- Business logic defines the rules for how your app functions and processes data.

- DeepAgent can automate complex business logic, including validation and notification systems.

- Properly configured business logic ensures that your app behaves as expected and handles edge cases.

5.3 Authentication and Authorization Workflows

Understanding Authentication and Authorization

- **Authentication**: The process of verifying the identity of a user (e.g., login with username and password).

- **Authorization**: The process of determining whether a user has permission to access specific resources (e.g., admin access, user privileges).

How DeepAgent Simplifies Authentication

DeepAgent can automate authentication logic, including generating login routes, verifying credentials, and creating tokens for session management.

Step-by-Step Process: Implementing Authentication

Prompting DeepAgent for User Authentication Flow

Example Prompt:

Create an authentication system for a task management app using JWT (JSON Web Tokens). The system should allow users to log in with email and password, and it should generate a token that can be used for accessing protected routes.

1. **Expected Output: Backend Authentication Code:**

```
const jwt = require("jsonwebtoken");

const bcrypt = require("bcryptjs");

const User = require("./models/User"); // Assuming a User model is defined


// User login route

app.post("/login", async (req, res) => {

  const { email, password } = req.body;

  const user = await User.findOne({ email });


  if (!user) {

    return res.status(400).send("Invalid email or password.");

  }


  const isMatch = await bcrypt.compare(password, user.password);

  if (!isMatch) {

    return res.status(400).send("Invalid email or password.");
```

```
}


// Generate JWT token

const token = jwt.sign({ userId: user._id }, "secretKey", { expiresIn: "1h" });

res.json({ token });

});


// Middleware to verify JWT token

function authenticate(req, res, next) {

  const token = req.headers["authorization"];

  if (!token) {

    return res.status(403).send("Access denied.");

  }


  jwt.verify(token, "secretKey", (err, decoded) => {

    if (err) {

      return res.status(403).send("Access denied.");

    }

    req.user = decoded;

    next();

  });
```

}

2. **Explanation of Code**:

- ○ **JWT generation**: After successful login, a JWT token is generated.

- ○ **Authentication middleware**: This middleware checks the token in the request headers and validates the user session.

Flowchart: Authentication Workflow

User Submits Credentials (Email & Password)

-> Validate Credentials (Check Database)

-> Password Match?

-> No -> Return Error (Invalid Credentials)

-> Yes -> Generate JWT Token

-> Return Token to User

-> Store Token in Client for Future Requests

Key Takeaways

- Authentication ensures that users can securely log in to your application.

- JWT tokens provide a way to securely manage user sessions.

- Authorization ensures that users can access only the resources they are permitted to.

5.4 Setting Up Webhooks and Event Handlers

What Are Webhooks and Event Handlers?

- **Webhooks**: A way for an application to send real-time updates to another application when certain events occur.

- **Event Handlers**: Functions that are triggered in response to specific events, like a database update or a user action.

How DeepAgent Helps with Webhooks

DeepAgent can help automate the configuration of webhooks, setting up HTTP endpoints that can listen for external events, process them, and trigger corresponding actions.

Step-by-Step Process: Configuring Webhooks

Prompting DeepAgent for Webhook Setup

Example Prompt:

Set up a webhook endpoint that listens for incoming notifications from a payment gateway. The webhook should handle events like payment success and failure, and update the user's account accordingly.

1. **Expected Output: Webhook Code Example**:

```javascript
const express = require("express");

const bodyParser = require("body-parser");

const app = express();



app.use(bodyParser.json());



// Webhook to handle payment gateway notifications

app.post("/webhook/payment", (req, res) => {

  const { event, data } = req.body;



  if (event === "payment_success") {

    // Update user account with successful payment

    const user = getUserById(data.userId);

    user.accountBalance += data.amount;

    user.save();

  } else if (event === "payment_failure") {

    // Notify user about the payment failure

    sendFailureNotification(data.userId);

  }
```

```
  res.status(200).send("Webhook received");

});


function getUserById(userId) {

  // Simulate fetching user from database

  return { id: userId, accountBalance: 1000, save: () => {} };

}


function sendFailureNotification(userId) {

  console.log(`Payment failed for user: ${userId}`);

}


app.listen(3000, () => console.log("Webhook server running"));
```

Explanation of Webhook Code:

- **Webhook listener**: A POST endpoint /webhook/payment listens for incoming events.

- **Event Processing**: Based on the event type (payment_success or payment_failure), different actions are taken.

- **Database Update**: For a successful payment, the user's balance is updated.

Flowchart: Webhook and Event Handling Workflow

Payment Gateway Sends Notification

  -> Webhook Receives Notification

    -> Event Type: "payment_success"?

      -> Yes -> Update User Account Balance

      -> No -> Handle Payment Failure

        -> Send Failure Notification

Key Takeaways

- Webhooks enable real-time communication between systems, reducing the need for polling.

- Event handlers trigger specific actions in your backend when an event occurs (e.g., a payment being processed).

- DeepAgent can help automate the creation of webhook endpoints and event handler logic.

5.5 Database Connection and ORM Configuration

What is ORM and Why Use It?

ORM (Object-Relational Mapping) bridges the gap between object-oriented programming and relational databases.

- **Benefits**:

    - Abstracts SQL queries with clean syntax

    - Provides model-based structure for database tables

    - Simplifies data manipulation and validation

Popular ORMs Used with DeepAgent Projects

ORM Tool	Language	Use Case
Prisma	TypeScript	Modern, type-safe database access
Sequelize	Node.js	Widely used, supports SQL dialects

TypeORM	TypeScript	Decorator-based, integrates well with TS
SQLAlchemy	Python	Powerful and flexible for complex queries

DeepAgent often selects Prisma or Sequelize when generating Node-based apps.

Step-by-Step: Connecting to a Database in DeepAgent

1. Prompting DeepAgent for ORM Setup

Example Prompt:

Set up a PostgreSQL database connection using Sequelize ORM for a task management app. Include user and task models.

---

2. DeepAgent Output: Configuration Snippet

```
// db.js - Sequelize initialization

const { Sequelize } = require("sequelize");

const sequelize = new Sequelize("taskapp", "username", "password", {

  host: "localhost",

  dialect: "postgres",
```

```
});
```

```
module.exports = sequelize;
```

Explanation:

- "taskapp" is the database name.

- "username" and "password" are your DB credentials.

- "postgres" sets the SQL dialect.

---

3. Defining Models with ORM

```js
// models/User.js

const { DataTypes } = require("sequelize");

const sequelize = require("../db");


const User = sequelize.define("User", {

  name: DataTypes.STRING,

  email: DataTypes.STRING,

});


module.exports = User;
```

```
// models/Task.js

const { DataTypes } = require("sequelize");

const sequelize = require("../db");


const Task = sequelize.define("Task", {

 title: DataTypes.STRING,

 completed: DataTypes.BOOLEAN,

});


module.exports = Task;
```

Flowchart: ORM Configuration Workflow

Developer Prompts DeepAgent

  -> DeepAgent Configures DB Connection

    -> Sets Up Sequelize or Prisma

      -> Defines Models (User, Task, etc.)

        -> Models Sync to Database

Best Practices for ORM Configuration

- Use environment variables for DB credentials (.env file)

- Sync models with the database using migrations or sequelize.sync()

- Validate model schemas for data consistency

Common Troubleshooting Tips

Issue	Solution
Authentication error	Check DB username/password and host
Dialect not supported	Ensure correct dialect (e.g., postgres, mysql)
Tables not created	Call sequelize.sync() in main server file
Circular imports	Use index.js to re-export models

Recap Table

Concept	Description	Tool Used
DB Connection	Connects app to database	Sequelize
ORM Models	Represent database tables as JavaScript/TypeScript code	Sequelize ORM
Model Sync	Ensures model definitions reflect in actual database	sequelize.sync()

Key Takeaways

- DeepAgent can auto-generate ORM setup code based on your prompt.

- Sequelize and Prisma are top choices for Node-based backend apps.

- ORM simplifies interactions with databases, improving maintainability.

Chapter 6: Designing the Frontend with AI Assistance

6.1 Choosing a Frontend Stack (React, Vue, etc.)

Why the Frontend Stack Matters

- Determines how users interact with your app.

- Impacts performance, scalability, and developer productivity.

- Influences how AI agents generate UI components.

Comparison Table: Frontend Frameworks

Framework	Language	Pros	Ideal For
React	JavaScript	Ecosystem-rich, widely supported, reusable	SPAs, dashboards, large-scale
Vue	JavaScript	Lightweight, easy to learn	Quick prototypes, small apps

Svelte	JavaScript	Fast and minimal boilerplate	Low-resource environments
Angular	TypeScript	Robust, full-featured	Enterprise-level apps

How DeepAgent Adapts Based on Stack Choice

- **React**: Generates JSX components, uses useState, useEffect, axios.

- **Vue**: Uses <template>, data, and methods structure.

- **Svelte**: Outputs reactive components with clean syntax.

- **Angular**: Generates modules, services, and component classes.

Text-Based Flowchart: Frontend Stack Decision Process

Need full control and ecosystem? -> Choose React

   |

  --> Want simple syntax and easy learning? -> Choose Vue

    |

   --> Need lightweight build? -> Choose Svelte

     |

    --> Prefer structured enterprise-level tooling? -> Choose Angular

Best Practices When Choosing a Stack

- Stick with **React** if unsure — DeepAgent defaults to it.

- Consider your **team's expertise**.

- Choose a **stack with strong community support**.

Key Takeaways

- The frontend stack influences how DeepAgent generates UI components.

- React is the most common and best-supported option.

- Vue and Svelte are lighter alternatives for simpler projects.

6.2 Generating UI Components with DeepAgent

Prompting DeepAgent for UI Generation

Example Prompt:

Generate a React login component with email and password fields, including error validation.

Sample Output from DeepAgent (React)

// LoginForm.jsx

```jsx
import React, { useState } from "react";

function LoginForm() {

  const [email, setEmail] = useState("");

  const [password, setPassword] = useState("");

  const [error, setError] = useState("");


  const handleSubmit = (e) => {

    e.preventDefault();

    if (!email || !password) {

      setError("All fields are required.");

    }

    // Call backend API

  };


  return (

    <form onSubmit={handleSubmit}>

      <input type="email" value={email} onChange={e => setEmail(e.target.value)}
placeholder="Email" />

      <input type="password" value={password} onChange={e => setPassword(e.target.value)}
placeholder="Password" />

      {error && <p>{error}</p>}
```

```
    <button type="submit">Login</button>

  </form>

 );

}


export default LoginForm;
```

DeepAgent Component Workflow

Prompt Input

  -> DeepAgent parses UI intent

    -> Selects stack (e.g., React)

      -> Generates HTML + JS logic

        -> Integrates state + validation

Table: Typical UI Components DeepAgent Can Generate

Component	Features Included	Frameworks Supported
Login Form	Fields, error messages, state	React, Vue, Angular

Dashboard Panel	Dynamic data, cards, charts	React, Vue
Modal Dialog	Visibility toggle, styling hooks	React, Svelte
CRUD Table	Pagination, filtering, sorting	React, Angular

Tips for High-Quality UI Prompts

- Be specific: Mention **fields**, **states**, and **events**.

- Use real-world context: e.g., "task manager dashboard" vs. "dashboard."

- Refine output by asking for **modularity** or **component reuse**.

Recap Table

Task	Prompt Strategy	Expected Output
Login Component	Fields + validation	Form with useState and handler
Dynamic Table	Fields + filters	Table with pagination and actions

| Dashboard UI | Widgets + layout | Grid-based layout with data charts |

Key Takeaways

- DeepAgent uses AI to interpret prompts and generate code-based UI.

- Prompt specificity increases quality and functionality.

- Generated components can be extended and customized easily.

6.3 Data Binding and State Management

Understanding Data Binding

- **One-Way Binding**: Data flows from component state to the UI.

- **Two-Way Binding**: Data flows both ways — changes in the UI update the component's state and vice versa.

State Management Concepts

Term	Description	Example

useState	React hook to manage local component state	const [value, setValue]
useEffect	Side effects like data fetching or syncing	useEffect(() => {}, [])
Context API	For sharing state globally across components	Theme, user session
Redux / Zustand	Advanced state management solutions	App-wide state handling

Sample: One-Way vs Two-Way Binding in React

One-Way Binding:

<input value={name} />

Two-Way Binding:

<input value={name} onChange={(e) => setName(e.target.value)} />

Text-Based Flowchart: Data Binding in DeepAgent UIs

User Input -> onChange Event -> Update State via setState -> UI Re-Renders -> User Sees Updated View

---

Common State Management Patterns with DeepAgent

- Form handling

- Modal visibility toggles

- API response storage

- Local/global cache for performance

Tips for Effective State Handling

- Use **local state** for isolated UI interactions.

- Use **global state** (e.g., Context) for authentication, theming, or user preferences.

- Avoid unnecessary state duplication.

Key Takeaways

- Proper state management ensures responsive and interactive UI.

- DeepAgent generates state hooks but understanding context improves customization.

- Two-way binding is essential for dynamic forms and inputs.

6.4 Handling Forms, Tables, and Dynamic Inputs

Working with Forms

- Forms are auto-generated with:

    - Input validation

    - State management

    - Submission handlers

Example: Login Form Logic

```
const handleLogin = (e) => {

  e.preventDefault();

  if (!email || !password) {

    setError("All fields required.");

  } else {

    api.post("/login", { email, password });

  }
```

```
};
```

Validation Logic Example

Field	Rule	Validation Code
Email	Must be valid email	/^[\w-\.]+@([\w-]+\.)+[\w-]{2,4}$/
Password	Min 6 chars	password.length >= 6

Building Interactive Tables

DeepAgent Features:

- Auto-generates tables with:

    - Pagination

    - Sorting

    - Action buttons (Edit/Delete)

Sample Code: Table Component

```
{data.map(item => (

  <tr key={item.id}>

    <td>{item.name}</td>

    <td>{item.status}</td>

    <td><button onClick={() => editItem(item.id)}>Edit</button></td>

  </tr>

))}
```

Dynamic Inputs Example

- Add/remove input fields

- Dynamic filtering/search

- Real-time previews (Markdown, forms, JSON)

Code Snippet: Dynamic Field List

```
{fields.map((field, index) => (

  <input key={index} value={field} onChange={e => updateField(index, e.target.value)} />

))}

<button onClick={addField}>Add Field</button>
```

Flowchart: Dynamic Form Handling

User Clicks "Add Field"

↓

New Input Field Rendered

↓

User Types Data

↓

onChange Triggers setState

↓

Updated Field Value Stored

Recap Table

Feature	DeepAgent Output Includes	Customization Tip
Form Component	Input fields, validation, submit handlers	Add onBlur for extra validation
Table Component	Data rows, pagination, sort, action buttons	Customize with filters or group logic

Dynamic Inputs	Controlled inputs with map() and state	Use array state and .map() in JSX

Key Takeaways

- Forms and tables are intelligently generated with built-in functionality.

- Dynamic inputs make apps highly customizable and user-friendly.

- Understanding state management ensures better control over user input and UI behavior.

6.5 Styling and Responsive Design Best Practices

1. Styling Strategies in DeepAgent Projects

DeepAgent typically integrates with popular CSS frameworks or utilities such as:

- **Tailwind CSS**

- **Bootstrap**

- **Styled Components (React)**

Styling Approach	Use Case	Pros
Utility-First (Tailwind)	Fast prototyping and AI-generated UIs	Fast, responsive, minimal
Component-Based (CSS-in-JS)	Customizable UI elements	Scoped, modular styling
Framework-Based (Bootstrap)	Standardized layout, mobile-first	Quick layout setup

2. Best Practices for Styling

- **Use utility classes** for consistency and predictability.

- **Avoid inline styles** unless dynamically required.

- **Define a design system** (colors, spacing, typography).

3. Responsive Design Techniques

Key Principles:

- Mobile-first development

- Flexbox and Grid usage

- Breakpoints for different screen sizes

Sample Flowchart: Responsive Design Strategy

Define Mobile Layout

↓

Use Flex/Grid to Arrange Elements

↓

Apply Media Queries (Tailwind: sm, md, lg)

↓

Test on Multiple Devices

---

4. Common Responsive Classes (Tailwind Example)

Class	Description
flex, grid	Layout containers
w-full, max-w	Width handling

sm:, md:, lg:	Media query prefixes
text-sm, text-lg	Responsive text sizes

5. Accessibility Considerations

- Use semantic HTML tags (<button>, <form>, <label>)

- Add ARIA roles where needed

- Ensure color contrast for readability

Key Takeaways

- Use a consistent styling approach tied to your chosen frontend framework.

- Build with mobile responsiveness in mind using modern layout tools.

- Focus on accessibility for wider usability.

6.6 Frontend Framework Recommendations for AI-Powered Apps

Top Frameworks for AI-Integrated Apps

Framework	Strengths	Ideal For
React	Component-based, AI-friendly, rich ecosystem	DeepAgent-generated UIs, SPAs
Vue.js	Simple learning curve, good integrations	Lightweight AI dashboards
Next.js	React + SSR/SSG for speed + SEO	AI apps with dynamic + static needs
Svelte	Minimal runtime, highly reactive	Performance-critical AI apps
Angular	Enterprise support, structured	Large-scale internal AI tools

Framework Comparison Table

Feature	React	Vue	Next.js	Svelte	Angular
Learning Curve	Medium	Easy	Medium	Easy	High
SSR Support	Yes (via Next)	Yes	Built-in	Limited	Yes
Ecosystem Size	Large	Medium	Large	Growing	Mature
AI/LLM Integration	Excellent	Good	Excellent	Moderate	Good

Best Practices for Choosing a Framework

1. **Start with React or Next.js** if you're unsure — they work best with AI-generated components.

2. Consider **Vue.js** for simplicity or **Svelte** for speed.

3. Use **Angular** only if you need a highly structured, enterprise-level tool.

Text-Based Decision Flowchart

Need SEO + Server-Side Rendering?

  └── Yes → Use Next.js

  └── No → Is simplicity important?

      └── Yes → Use Vue.js or Svelte

      └── No → Use React or Angular

Key Takeaways

- React and Next.js are the most compatible with DeepAgent-generated code.

- Framework choice should align with project complexity, performance needs, and developer skill level.

- Consider future maintainability and available UI libraries when selecting a stack.

Chapter 7: Automation Workflows and AI Integration

7.1 Understanding DeepAgent's Automation Capabilities

---

1. What is Automation in DeepAgent?

Automation in DeepAgent refers to:

- **Automated backend logic** triggered by events

- **AI-enhanced workflows** that make decisions or process data

- **Scheduled tasks** like data sync, email triggers, report generation

---

2. Key Capabilities

Feature	Description	Use Case Example
Event-Driven Logic	Automate responses to events (e.g., user signup)	Send welcome emails automatically
AI Workflow Nodes	Use LLMs inside workflows to make decisions or summarize data	Auto-generate reports from raw data

Multi-Step Workflows	Chain multiple operations in a single flow	Approve document → Notify user → Store
Condition-Based Branching	Add logic gates in automation flows	If user premium → Trigger premium flow

3. Flowchart: Automation Workflow Example

User Submits Form

↓

Validate Input with AI

↓

If Valid:

→ Store in Database

→ Send Confirmation Email

Else:

→ Trigger Error Notification

4. Integration Points for AI

- Use LLMs in:

    - Input validation

    - Text summarization

    - Decision trees (Yes/No, Prioritization)

5. Summary Table

Automation Element	Description	AI Enhancement
Triggers	Start automation via events or time	Classify intent of trigger
Actions	Execute steps like API calls	Summarize data for output
Conditions	Decision points	Use LLM for branching logic

Key Takeaways

- Automation in DeepAgent saves time and reduces errors.

- AI can enhance automation flows by bringing decision-making to non-human steps.

- Building intelligent workflows requires combining triggers, logic, and AI tools.

7.2 Trigger-Based Workflows and Scheduling

1. What Are Triggers?

Triggers are events that **start workflows** in DeepAgent. They can be:

- **User Events** (e.g., form submission)

- **System Events** (e.g., database update)

- **Scheduled Events** (e.g., every day at 9 AM)

2. Common Trigger Types

Trigger Type	Description	Example
Webhook	Triggered by external HTTP request	Stripe payment confirmation
Time-Based	Runs on a schedule (cron-style)	Nightly data backup

App Event	Triggers from DeepAgent app logic	User logs in
Conditional	Runs when a condition is met	User score > 80 → Send certificate

---

3. Setting Up Triggers

Step-by-Step Guide:

1. **Define Trigger**: Choose from event, time, or webhook.

2. **Attach Workflow**: Link to the action or logic to execute.

3. **Test Trigger**: Simulate or invoke the trigger manually.

4. **Monitor Logs**: Verify that the workflow was triggered successfully.

---

4. Flowchart: Trigger-Based Scheduling Logic

Scheduled Trigger (Daily at 8 AM)

↓

Query Database for Pending Tasks

↓

If Tasks Exist:

→ Process Tasks

→ Send Notifications

Else:

→ Log "No Tasks Found"

5. Time-Based Scheduling Syntax (Crontab-like)

Schedule	Cron Format	Meaning
Every minute	* * * * *	Run every minute
Daily at 9 AM	0 9 * * *	Run once per day at 9 AM
Every Monday	0 10 * * 1	Run weekly on Monday at 10 AM

Key Takeaways

- Triggers are the starting points of automated, intelligent workflows.

- DeepAgent supports webhook, system, and scheduled triggers.

- Scheduling allows for predictable, timed automation that enhances app performance.

7.3 Integrating LLMs into Your App Workflows

---

1. Why Use LLMs in Workflows?

LLMs add reasoning and natural language processing capabilities to your automations. They can:

- Interpret user inputs

- Generate dynamic responses

- Analyze large text blocks

- Make decisions based on context

---

2. Common Use Cases

Use Case	LLM Role	Workflow Example

Ticket Classification	Categorize issues from text	Tag support tickets with urgency
Email Summarization	Summarize customer messages	Provide agent with a digest before response
Recommendation Engine	Suggest actions or products	Suggest next best action after user interaction
Intent Recognition	Detect user intent from messages	Route to appropriate service or team

3. Integration Steps (Step-by-Step)

1. **Identify Workflow Context**
   e.g., User submits a support request via form

2. **Add LLM Node or Block**
   Use DeepAgent's LLM integration node

Define Prompt Template
Example:

Classify this support request by category and urgency:

"{{user_message}}"

3. **Process Output**

   Parse and route the result:

   - If "urgent", notify team

   - If "billing", assign to finance

---

4. Flowchart: LLM-Enhanced Workflow Example

User Submits Support Message

   ↓

 LLM Classifies Request

   ↓

 → If "Urgent": Notify Support Team

 → If "General": Auto-Reply with FAQ

---

5. Prompt Engineering Tips

- Provide clear, direct instructions.

- Use delimiters (like """) to mark input.

- Add few-shot examples if needed for consistency.

Key Takeaways

- LLMs enable intelligent automation beyond hard-coded rules.

- DeepAgent allows seamless integration of LLMs in workflow steps.

- Clear prompt engineering is key to reliable outputs.

7.4 Intelligent Decision Making Using AI Agents

1. What is Intelligent Decision-Making?

It's the process of letting an AI agent:

- Analyze a situation

- Evaluate multiple options

- Choose the best course of action

- Execute or recommend based on context

2. Components of an AI Agent in a Workflow

Component	Description	Example

Perception Layer	Gathers data from the environment	User input, API data
Decision Logic	Determines the next action	If X > 50, trigger Y
Action Layer	Executes commands or returns outputs	Send email, update DB, call API

3. Flowchart: AI Agent Decision System

Data Input (User Interaction, Sensor, API)

↓

AI Agent Evaluates Context

↓

→ Option A → Meets Criteria → Execute A

→ Option B → Else → Execute B

4. Practical Examples

1. **Loan Approval Workflow**

- AI agent reviews credit score, income, and employment

- Approves or flags based on scoring thresholds

2. **Support Routing**

- LLM detects tone and urgency

- Agent routes to appropriate department

3. **Dynamic Pricing**

- AI agent adjusts pricing based on inventory and demand

5. Logic Tables: Decision Conditions

Condition	Decision	Action
Sentiment = Negative	Escalate to Human Agent	Notify via Slack
User Plan = Premium	Provide Live Support Option	Start Chatbot Session
Order Total > $500	Apply Priority Shipping	Modify Order in DB

Key Takeaways

- AI agents can perform complex, real-time decisions.

- Logic can be driven by LLM output, structured data, or external APIs.

- DeepAgent simplifies AI agent orchestration with workflow nodes.

7.5 Auto-Summarization, Chatbots, and Natural Language Interfaces

1. Overview of Capabilities

These features allow users to interact with your application in human-like ways and consume information efficiently.

Feature	Description	Use Case Example
Auto-Summarization	Condenses large content into key points	Summarize reports, emails, meeting transcripts
Chatbots (Conversational UI)	Responds to queries, guides users, performs actions	Customer support, onboarding assistant
NL Interfaces	Lets users query and control systems using natural language	"Show me today's orders" becomes an SQL query

2. Auto-Summarization with LLMs

How It Works:

1. Text block is passed to an LLM.

2. Prompt defines the tone and length of the summary.

3. LLM returns condensed, structured information.

Prompt Example:

Summarize the following customer feedback into 3 bullet points with key insights:

"""

The customer found the onboarding difficult but appreciated the support staff. The UI was slow to load...

"""

Flowchart:

Input Text → LLM Summarizes → Output: Concise Bullets/Paragraph

Integration Steps:

1. Capture long-form content (e.g., support ticket).

2. Send to LLM with summarization prompt.

3. Display or store summary in database or UI.

---

3. Building Chatbots with DeepAgent

Types of Chatbots:

- **FAQ bots**: Answer predefined questions.

- **Smart bots**: Use context and LLMs to generate responses.

- **Action bots**: Execute tasks based on commands.

Architecture Flow:

User Input → Intent Detection (LLM) → Action Engine → Response

Example Workflow:

1. User types: "Reset my password."

2. LLM detects intent: reset_password.

3. DeepAgent triggers the appropriate backend function.

Prompting Strategy:

- Provide examples in prompts.

- Define action-response pairs.

- Use memory/state when required for context.

---

4. Natural Language Interfaces (NLUI)

Concept:

Users control backend systems by typing natural language, which is translated into structured queries or commands.

Examples:

- Input: "List all pending invoices."

- Translated: SELECT * FROM invoices WHERE status = 'pending';

Workflow:

NL Input → LLM Parses Intent & Entities → Structured Command → Execute → Result Displayed

Table: Common Inputs and Generated Queries

Natural Language Input	SQL Command Generated
"Show users registered today"	SELECT * FROM users WHERE created_at = CURRENT_DATE;

"Top 5 products by sales"	SELECT product, SUM(sales) FROM orders GROUP BY product ORDER BY SUM(sales) DESC LIMIT 5;

5. Best Practices

- Use **prompt chaining**: One LLM call for intent, another for query generation.

- Validate outputs before execution for security.

- Keep logs of user queries and LLM interpretations for debugging.

Key Takeaways

- Auto-summarization reduces cognitive load and enhances productivity.

- Chatbots powered by LLMs make your app interactive and user-friendly.

- Natural language interfaces empower users to interact with data intuitively.

Chapter 8: Connecting with External Tools and APIs

8.1 Using Built-In DeepAgent Connectors

Overview of Built-In Connectors

DeepAgent includes plug-and-play integrations for common tools such as:

Connector Type	Examples	Use Case
CRM	Salesforce, HubSpot	Sync customer data
Messaging	Slack, Discord, Twilio	Send notifications or receive triggers
Email	Gmail, Outlook	Send summary reports
Databases	PostgreSQL, MongoDB, MySQL	Sync or query external datasets
Cloud Storage	AWS S3, Google Drive	Upload/download files from workflows

Step-by-Step: Setting Up a Connector

1. **Choose Connector**:

   o Navigate to the "Integrations" section.

   o Select the external tool (e.g., Slack).

2. **Authenticate**:

   o DeepAgent will prompt for OAuth login or API Key.

   o Tokens are securely stored in encrypted secrets.

3. **Map Actions**:

   o Choose what you want to do: e.g., "Send message to Slack."

   o Map it to an event: e.g., "On new record creation."

4. **Test and Activate**:

   o Use the testing sandbox to verify.

   o Deploy the workflow live.

Flowchart: Connector Integration

Trigger Event in DeepAgent

↓

Check Conditions

↓

Invoke External Connector

↓

Send/Receive Data

↓

Continue Workflow

Best Practices

- Use **connector logs** to debug errors or data mismatches.

- Always define **fallback paths** in case external API fails.

- Re-authenticate tokens periodically if required.

8.2 REST and GraphQL API Integrations

Why Use APIs?

- When no built-in connector exists.

- For deeper, more customized control.

- To connect with in-house systems.

REST Integration Steps

1. **Define the Endpoint**:

   o **Example:** https://api.example.com/orders

2. **Set Method and Headers**:

   o Method: GET, POST, PUT, DELETE

   o Headers: Authorization, Content-Type

3. **Input Payload**:

   o JSON body with variables from your app (e.g., user ID, product ID)

4. **Map Response**:

   o Use JSONPath or object destructuring to extract response fields.

   o Feed them into your database or UI.

GraphQL Integration Steps

Write Query or Mutation:

```
query GetUser {

 user(id: "123") {

  name

  email

 }

}
```

1. **Send Request:**

   - DeepAgent sends the GraphQL query to the endpoint.

2. **Handle Response:**

   - DeepAgent parses the response and updates data bindings.

Table: REST vs. GraphQL Comparison

Feature	REST	GraphQL
Data Fetching	Multiple endpoints	Single endpoint
Flexibility	Rigid	Highly customizable

Response Size	Larger (includes unused fields)	Smaller (you define fields)
Learning Curve	Low	Moderate

Tips for API Integration

- Use **environment variables** to store API keys and URLs securely.

- Limit response size for faster performance.

- Implement **rate limiting** where necessary to prevent throttling.

Key Takeaways

- DeepAgent's built-in connectors simplify common integrations.

- For custom needs, REST and GraphQL APIs give you full control.

- Properly structured APIs allow your app to scale and interact intelligently with other systems.

8.3 Working with Email, Slack, Notion, and Jira

Integration Scenarios

Tool	Use Case Example	DeepAgent Role
Email	Send reports, receive commands via inbox	Trigger/Action for automated email handling
Slack	Notify team on workflow success or error	Real-time alerts, slash commands
Notion	Create or update pages/databases dynamically	Auto-document project progress
Jira	Create/update issues based on bug reports	Manage project lifecycle using triggers

Connecting to Each Tool

Email Integration (SMTP/IMAP or Gmail API)

1. Go to **Integrations > Email** in DeepAgent.

2. Choose method: SMTP (send), IMAP (receive), or Gmail API.

3. Authenticate using OAuth or credentials.

4. Set trigger (e.g., new email with subject = "Create Ticket").

5. Map the payload to an internal workflow.

Slack Integration

1. Connect to Slack workspace via DeepAgent OAuth.

2. Choose channel and events:

    o   Trigger: New message in channel.

    o   Action: Post message, add reaction, send DM.

3. Define bot behavior using natural language prompts.

Notion Integration

1. Authenticate with Notion.

2. Choose database or page.

3. Define actions:

    o   Add new row to task DB.

    o   Update content of specific page.

4. DeepAgent reads Notion schemas and maps to entities.

Jira Integration

1. Connect via Jira API token and domain.

2. Configure triggers:

   o New bug assigned.

   o Task status change.

3. Use DeepAgent to:

   o Auto-create tickets from app errors.

   o Update status based on resolved tasks.

Example: Bug Report Workflow

User Reports Issue (Form Submission)

↓

DeepAgent Parses Issue Description

↓

Create Jira Ticket + Post to Slack Channel

↓

Add New Entry in Notion Project Tracker

↓

Send Confirmation Email to User

Tips for Productivity Tool Integration

- Create fallback flows for failed messages or API errors.

- Always verify permission scopes when integrating third-party tools.

- Use conditional logic to route actions differently based on severity (e.g., high-priority issues trigger SMS).

8.4 Web Scraping and Data Ingestion

Use Cases for Web Scraping and Ingestion

- Extract product data from competitor websites.

- Monitor public repositories for updates.

- Populate app dashboards with real-time news or metrics.

- Automate research or content generation workflows.

Data Ingestion Options in DeepAgent

Method	Description	When to Use
API Integration	Pull structured data from JSON/XML sources	Reliable sources with clear endpoints
Web Scraping	Extract data from HTML pages using CSS/XPath	Sites without public APIs
File Upload	CSV, Excel, or JSON upload for batch ingestion	Manual import of legacy or bulk data
RSS/Feeds	Monitor content feeds (blogs, news, etc.)	For regularly updated public data

Step-by-Step: Scraping with DeepAgent

1. **Define Target Page**:

o   Input target URL and user-agent header.

2. **Select Data Points**:

     o   Use CSS selectors or XPath expressions to extract fields.

3. **Clean and Transform**:

     o   Remove unwanted tags, convert types (e.g., string to number).

4. **Store in Database**:

     o   Map fields to your database schema or app entities.

Example Flow: Product Price Tracker

Daily Trigger (Scheduler)

↓

Scrape Product Page for Price + Availability

↓

Compare with Stored Data

↓

If Price Dropped -> Notify User via Email

Best Practices for Web Scraping

- Respect robots.txt and site scraping policies.

- Implement throttling/delays to avoid bans.

- Use dynamic scraping with headless browsers for JS-heavy sites (e.g., Puppeteer or Playwright integration).

- Regularly validate your selectors to ensure data accuracy.

Table: Ingestion Method Comparison

Method	Data Structure	Real-Time	Complexity	Maintenance
REST API	Structured	Yes	Low	Low
Web Scraping	Semi-structured	Sometimes	Medium	High
File Upload	Structured	No	Low	Low
RSS Feeds	Semi-structured	Yes	Low	Medium

Key Takeaways

- DeepAgent makes it easy to connect and automate across modern tools like Slack, Notion, and Jira.

- It also provides flexible scraping and ingestion mechanisms for integrating external data.

- Combined, these features allow developers to build intelligent, dynamic, and integrated systems with minimal manual effort.

8.5 Authentication with OAuth2 and API Keys

Understanding Authentication Methods

Method	Description	Use Case
API Key	A static string used to authenticate requests.	Simple integrations with trusted services.
OAuth2	A token-based flow allowing delegated access without sharing passwords.	Secure, scoped access to user accounts or third-party platforms.

DeepAgent Support for Authentication

Integration Type	Authentication Supported

REST APIs	API Key, OAuth2
SaaS Apps (Slack, Google)	OAuth2
Internal Tools	Basic Auth, API Keys

Flowchart: Authentication Workflow in DeepAgent

Developer Defines Integration

↓

Choose Auth Type (API Key or OAuth2)

↓

Configure Auth Settings (keys, scopes, endpoints)

↓

DeepAgent Stores Token/Key Securely

↓

Use in Workflow or Trigger Securely

1. Using API Keys in DeepAgent

Step-by-Step:

1. **Locate the API Key:**

   o From the third-party service dashboard (e.g., OpenWeatherMap, Mailchimp).

2. **Open DeepAgent Integration Settings.**

3. **Enter Key in Secure Field.**

4. **Test Connection.**

Use in Request Header or Query:

```
{

"headers": {

  "Authorization": "Bearer YOUR_API_KEY"

}

}
```

Tips:

- Rotate keys regularly.

- Never log keys or expose in frontend.

- Use environment variables for deployment.

2. OAuth2 Integration in DeepAgent

Common Use Cases: Slack, Google, Notion, GitHub, Dropbox.

Step-by-Step:

1. **Register Your App** on the service provider:

   o   Define redirect URL (https://deepagent.app/oauth/callback).

   o   Note your **Client ID** and **Client Secret**.

2. **Open DeepAgent > Integrations > OAuth2.**

3. **Fill Configuration:**

Field	Example Value
Auth URL	https://accounts.google.com/o/oauth2/auth
Token URL	https://oauth2.googleapis.com/token
Scopes	email, profile, https://www.googleapis.com/auth/drive
Redirect URI	Auto-filled by DeepAgent

4. **DeepAgent Handles Authorization Flow:**

- Redirects user to auth URL.

- Receives auth code and exchanges it for an access token.

Use Token in Workflow API Calls:

```
{

"headers": {

  "Authorization": "Bearer {{access_token}}"

}

}
```

Comparison Table: API Key vs OAuth2

Feature	API Key	OAuth2
Security Level	Basic	High (token-based with expiry/refresh)
Access Scope	Full access (usually)	Granular, scoped access
Best For	Internal APIs, trusted services	User-specific access to 3rd-party services

Expiration	Rarely expires	Tokens expire, require refresh
Ease of Setup	Easy	Moderate (requires app registration)

Security Best Practices

- Store credentials in **encrypted secrets manager** within DeepAgent.

- **Limit token scopes** to the minimum necessary.

- **Refresh OAuth tokens** automatically using DeepAgent's built-in token handler.

- **Avoid hardcoding** credentials in code or prompt templates.

Key Takeaways

- Use **API Keys** for fast, simple authentication with minimal complexity.

- Use **OAuth2** for secure, delegated access to user-based services.

- DeepAgent provides native support for both, with secure storage and token handling.

- Always follow security best practices when handling credentials in production environments.

Chapter 9: Testing and Debugging AI-Generated Code

9.1 Unit Testing and Integration Testing in AI-Generated Code

What is Unit Testing?

Unit testing is the practice of testing **individual functions or components** of an application in isolation.

- Focus: Single function/module

- Tools: Jest, Mocha, PyTest, etc.

What is Integration Testing?

Integration testing ensures **multiple modules** work together correctly.

- Focus: Interaction between components (e.g., API + Database)

- Tools: Supertest, Postman, Selenium, Cypress

Table: Comparison Between Unit and Integration Testing

Feature	Unit Testing	Integration Testing
Scope	Single function/module	Combined behavior of components
Speed	Very fast	Slower (depends on external systems)
Failure Debugging	Easy	Requires more context tracing
Best Used For	Logic validation	End-to-end data and service validation
Example Tool	Jest, PyTest	Postman, Supertest, Cypress

How DeepAgent Handles Tests

Area	AI Behavior	Test Integration
API Generation	Creates RESTful routes	Unit + Integration

Database Models	Defines schemas and constraints	Unit
Business Logic	Implements from prompts	Unit
UI Components	JSX or Vue code via LLM	Unit (component)

Flowchart: Testing Workflow for AI-Generated Code

Generate Code with DeepAgent

↓

Define Unit Tests (Logic/Functions)

↓

Mock External Dependencies (APIs, DB)

↓

Run Unit Tests and Fix Issues

↓

Create Integration Tests (Full Flow)

↓

Test Deployment Environment

Confirm Passes Before Shipping

Example: Unit Test for AI-Generated API Endpoint (Express + Jest)

```javascript
// userController.js

exports.getUser = (req, res) => {

  return res.status(200).json({ id: 1, name: "Jane Doe" });

};
```

```javascript
// userController.test.js

const { getUser } = require('./userController');

test('should return user with id and name', () => {

  const req = {};

  const res = {

    status: jest.fn(() => res),

    json: jest.fn(),

  };

  getUser(req, res);

  expect(res.status).toHaveBeenCalledWith(200);

  expect(res.json).toHaveBeenCalledWith({ id: 1, name: "Jane Doe" });

});
```

Best Practices for Testing AI-Generated Code

- Use **test-first or test-after** strategies to validate generated logic.

- Leverage **DeepAgent test scaffolds** (when available).

- Always **mock external APIs** to avoid instability.

- Maintain **a test coverage threshold** (e.g., 80%).

9.2 Debugging DeepAgent Outputs

Common Issues with AI-Generated Code

Issue Type	Description	Resolution Strategy
Incorrect Logic	AI misunderstood the requirement	Refine prompt, add constraints
Incomplete Code	AI stops generation early	Re-run prompt with specific output format
API Errors	Bad request/response format	Use logs and API validators

Frontend Integration	Data mismatch, missing props	Inspect state and component hierarchy
Database Connection	Config or ORM errors	Validate DSN, schema mapping

Step-by-Step Debugging Strategy

1. **Read Logs**:

    - Use DeepAgent's logging console or browser dev tools.

2. **Check Input Prompts**:

    - Refactor ambiguous phrasing.

    - Add examples to prompt for clearer intent.

3. **Validate Output Code**:

    - Run linters and formatters (e.g., ESLint, Prettier).

4. **Test API Routes**:

    - Use curl, Postman, or built-in test tools.

5. **Inspect Data Flow**:

    - Trace variables from input → state → output.

Table: Debugging Toolkit

Tool	Purpose
Console Logs	Quick runtime inspection
Postman	API call testing
ESLint/Prettier	Code quality and formatting
DeepAgent Logs	Errors during code or logic generation
Jest/Chai	Assertion and test failures
DB Clients	Validate database connection and queries

Key Takeaways

- AI-generated code must be **tested like human-written code**.

- Combine **unit and integration tests** to ensure functionality and reliability.

- Use **structured debugging practices** to correct logic or generation flaws.

- Effective **prompt engineering** is critical for avoiding repeated errors.

- DeepAgent provides support tools, but manual verification is essential for quality **Apps**assurance.

9.3 Validating API Responses and Database Queries

1. Validating API Responses

Step-by-Step Process:

1. **Use a Testing Tool**:

   - Examples: Postman, curl, REST Client (VSCode), Insomnia

2. **Send Request to API Endpoint**:

   - E.g., GET /api/users/1

3. **Check Response Details**:

   - Status Code (e.g., 200 OK)

   - Headers (Content-Type, etc.)

   - Body (data returned)

Expected Validation Flow:

Send API Request

↓

Receive Status Code → Should be 2xx or 4xx

↓

Validate Headers → e.g., Content-Type: application/json

↓

Check Response Body → Match structure & values

Table: Key API Response Components to Validate

Component	Description	Example
Status Code	HTTP code indicating result	200 OK, 404 Not Found
Content-Type	Response data format	application/json
Body	Main data payload	{ "id": 1, "name": "Jane" }

Schema	Structure validation (optional w/ tools)	Joi, Zod, OpenAPI Spec

---

2. Validating Database Queries

Options for Validation:

- Use an **ORM console** (e.g., Prisma, Sequelize, TypeORM).

- Run **raw SQL** in a client like DBeaver, pgAdmin, or MySQL Workbench.

- Use DeepAgent's logs or internal query trace (if exposed).

Example: Verifying Insert Query

1. DeepAgent generates code to insert a user.

2. Run the operation in-app or via API.

3. Use SELECT * FROM users WHERE id = 1; to confirm result.

Validation Checklist

- ✓ Correct data inserted/updated/deleted?

- ☑ All required fields handled?

- ☑ Relationships preserved (e.g., foreign keys)?

- ☑ Indexes used? (Performance check)

- ☑ No duplication or data loss?

9.4 Common Pitfalls and How to Fix Them

1. Misaligned Data Structures

Problem: The frontend expects { name, age } but backend returns { username, years_old }.

Fix:

- Align your schema and UI expectations.

- Use a schema validator or response mapper.

2. Missing Authentication Headers

Problem: API requests return 401 Unauthorized.

Fix:

- Ensure JWT or API keys are attached.

- Use middleware (Express example):

```
app.use((req, res, next) => {

  const token = req.headers['authorization'];

  if (!token) return res.sendStatus(401);

  // validate token logic

  next();

});
```

3. ORM Connection Failures

Problem: App cannot connect to the database.

Fix:

- Double-check environment variables.

- Ensure database is running and accessible.

- Test connection manually:

```
psql -h localhost -U user -d mydb
```

4. Incorrect Prompt Output

Problem: DeepAgent misunderstood the user intent and generated flawed logic.

Fix:

- Rephrase the prompt with specifics.

- Add example outputs.

- Break tasks into smaller subtasks.

5. Race Conditions or Timing Errors

Problem: Async operations complete out of order, causing UI or data errors.

Fix:

- Use async/await or proper promise chaining.

- Avoid relying on time-based logic.

Table: Common Pitfalls and Solutions

Pitfall	Description	Fix
Schema Mismatch	Frontend & backend expect different fields	Normalize schema or use mappers

Missing Headers	Auth or CORS headers not present	Add headers in frontend & backend config
ORM Not Connecting	Wrong DB config	Validate env vars and DSN string
LLM Misinterpretation	Prompt not specific enough	Refine or break down the prompt
Asynchronous Errors	Unhandled promises or timing bugs	Use await, Promise.all, error checks

Key Takeaways

- Always test API responses against expected structure and status codes.

- Validate database state post-operation to ensure data integrity.

- Use the right tools (Postman, SQL clients) and logic checks to debug.

- Most issues can be traced to **prompt quality**, **data mismatches**, or **config errors**.

- Apply structured testing and validation to reduce risk in AI-generated apps.

9.5 Implementing Continuous Feedback Loops with AI

What is a Feedback Loop in AI-Powered Development?

A **feedback loop** is a cycle where outputs or outcomes are continuously monitored, analyzed, and used to improve future system performance.

Flowchart: Feedback Loop Process

User Interacts with App

↓

Log Activity and Capture User Feedback

↓

Analyze Behavior and Output Accuracy

↓

Adjust Prompts / Retrain Models / Improve Logic

↓

Regenerate or Update Code

↓

Deploy Improved Version

↓

(Loop repeats)

Types of Feedback to Capture

Source	Description	Example
User Behavior	How users interact with the app	Clicks, form inputs, navigation patterns
Error Reports	Automated logs or manual error feedback	500 errors, stack traces
Prompt Failures	When AI output does not match expectations	Wrong schema generated, incorrect logic
Manual Ratings	Human reviews or evaluations	👍 / 👎 on chatbot responses

Step-by-Step Guide: Building a Feedback Loop in DeepAgent-Generated Apps

1. **Instrument Your App**
   Add logging or analytics to record:

   - API request/response cycles

- Errors

- User actions

2. **Capture Structured Feedback**

   - Add UI elements for user ratings/comments.

Log usage data in a feedback table:

```
CREATE TABLE feedback (

id SERIAL PRIMARY KEY,

component TEXT,

feedback_type TEXT,

message TEXT,

timestamp TIMESTAMP DEFAULT CURRENT_TIMESTAMP

);
```

3. **Analyze Feedback Regularly**

   - Use analytics or dashboards to identify trends.

   - Export and inspect prompt failures or inconsistencies.

4. **Update Prompts and Logic**

   - Refine AI prompts based on observed weaknesses.

- Example: If AI consistently mislabels fields, add examples or use constraints in prompts.

5. **Revalidate and Re-deploy**

   - Regenerate the updated logic using DeepAgent.

   - Run regression tests before deploying.

6. **Document Learnings**

   - Maintain a feedback changelog.

   - Helps trace cause/effect across iterations.

Example: Feedback Loop for an Auto-Generated Chatbot

Step	Implementation Example
Log User Input	Save to chat_logs table
Analyze Misunderstood Inputs	Identify intents the model failed to understand
Refine Prompt	Add more examples or clarify intent descriptions
Re-generate Chat Logic	Use DeepAgent to create updated bot logic

Test and Re-deploy	Validate the new behavior, then redeploy

Tip

Continuous feedback loops allow you to turn real-world usage into continuous improvement without requiring full code rewrites.

Best Practices

- **Start small**: Begin with basic logging and user ratings before scaling into full analytics.

- **Automate analysis**: Use cron jobs or background tasks to process feedback data.

- **Avoid overfitting**: Don't over-adjust prompts based on isolated cases—look for consistent patterns.

- **Create a feedback schema**: Define clear structures for what feedback data to collect and how.

Summary Table: Key Components of Feedback Loop

Component	Purpose	Tools/Methods

Logging	Track system behavior	Winston, LogRocket, server logs
Feedback Storage	Store user/system input	SQL, NoSQL tables
Analytics	Find patterns and weak points	Superset, Grafana, DeepAgent reports
Prompt Tuning	Improve AI responses	Prompt engineering
Automation	Streamline loop implementation	CRON jobs, background workers

Key Takeaways

- Feedback loops are critical for **AI-powered apps** to remain effective and user-centered.

- Combining **manual** and **automated** feedback allows for continual refinement.

- DeepAgent's outputs can be improved not only through better prompts but also by incorporating **user behavior insights**.

- Treat feedback as an evolving dataset that powers your product's learning curve.

Chapter 10: Deployment and Maintenance

10.1 Exporting and Hosting Your Application

Exporting from DeepAgent

When your application is complete, DeepAgent typically offers an **export option** (CLI or Web UI) to generate the complete codebase.

Step-by-Step: Exporting Your Project

Generate the Final Build

Use the platform's UI or CLI to export:

```
deepagent export --project "my-app"
```

1. **Review the Project Structure**

```
    my-app/
├── backend/
│   ├── api/
│   ├── models/
│   └── database/
├── frontend/
│   ├── components/
```

```
|   └── pages/

├── .env.example

├── docker-compose.yml

└── README.md
```

2. **Configure Environment Variables**

   Create a .env file with production credentials:

   DATABASE_URL=postgres://user:password@host:5432/dbname

SECRET_KEY=your-secret

3. **Prepare for Hosting**

   o   Ensure CORS, SSL, and error-handling middleware are configured.

Test locally with:

npm run build && npm start

Flowchart: Hosting Prep Process

Export Project -> Review & Clean Code -> Set .env and Secrets

   ↓

Configure Dependencies -> Choose Host (Vercel, Docker, etc.)

   ↓

Deploy -> Monitor Logs & Errors -> Iterate

Hosting Options Comparison

Platform	Backend Support	Frontend Support	Scaling	Ideal For
Vercel	Limited via Serverless	Full	Auto	Static/SSR Frontends
Heroku	Full (Dynos)	Full	Medium	Quick MVPs
Render	Full	Full	Auto	Full-stack Web Apps
AWS/GCP/Azure	Full (manual)	Full	High	Enterprise-grade systems

10.2 Deployment with Docker, Vercel, and Heroku

Option 1: Docker Deployment

Docker enables **portable deployment** of your application by containerizing it.

Step-by-Step: Docker Deployment

Write a Dockerfile

```
FROM node:18

WORKDIR /app

COPY . .

RUN npm install

RUN npm run build

CMD ["npm", "start"]
```

1. **Build and Run Locally**

```
docker build -t my-app .
```

```
docker run -p 3000:3000 --env-file .env my-app
```

2. **Optional**: Use docker-compose.yml for multi-service apps (e.g., backend + database).

Option 2: Deploying to Vercel

Vercel is ideal for **frontend** and **serverless** deployment.

Steps:

1. Push project to **GitHub**.

2. Go to vercel.com, connect your GitHub repo.

Configure **build commands**:

Build: npm run build

Output directory: dist or .vercel/output

3. Set environment variables in Vercel dashboard.

4. Click **Deploy**.

Option 3: Deploying to Heroku

Heroku supports both frontend and backend deployments with Git integration.

Steps:

Install Heroku CLI:

npm install -g heroku

1. Initialize Git and push:

git init

heroku create my-ai-app

git add . && git commit -m "Deploy"

git push heroku master

2. Add environment variables:

   heroku config:set DATABASE_URL=...

3. Monitor logs:

   heroku logs --tail

Table: Feature Comparison

Feature	Docker	Vercel	Heroku
Custom Backend Support	✓	✗ (serverless)	✓
Database Integration	✓	External only	✓ (Postgres)
CI/CD Support	✓	✓	✓
Complexity	Medium	Low	Low
Cost (Startup)	Free Tier	Free Tier	Free Tier

Best Practices

- **Secure Your Environment**: Use .env for secrets—never hardcode sensitive values.

- **Monitor Performance**: Use built-in logging or tools like LogRocket, Sentry.

- **Use CI/CD Pipelines**: Automate testing and deployment using GitHub Actions or similar tools.

Key Takeaways

- Exporting from DeepAgent provides a complete, deployable codebase.

- Docker offers flexibility for any hosting environment.

- Vercel is best for frontend-first, serverless setups.

- Heroku remains ideal for quick full-stack deployments with simple setup.

- Always review and sanitize AI-generated code before deployment.

10.3 Managing Database Migrations

What Are Database Migrations?

Migrations are version-controlled files that **alter the database schema**—such as adding tables, changing columns, or creating relationships—while keeping track of historical changes.

Why Migrations Matter

Benefit	Description
Version Control	Migrations act as a changelog for your database.
Team Collaboration	Shared migration files help sync databases across dev environments.
Rollback Support	Changes can be reversed safely.
CI/CD Integration	Migrations can be run automatically during deployment.

Popular Migration Tools

Stack	Tool	Command Example
Node.js	Prisma	npx prisma migrate dev
Python	Alembic	alembic upgrade head
PHP/Laravel	Artisan	php artisan migrate

Django	Migrate	python manage.py migrate
Rails	ActiveRecord	rails db:migrate

Step-by-Step: Managing Migrations with Prisma (Node.js)

Create a Model in schema.prisma

```
model User {

id   Int    @id @default(autoincrement())

name  String

email String  @unique

}
```

1. **Run the Migration Command**

   ```
   npx prisma migrate dev --name init
   ```

2. **Apply Changes to Production**

   ```
   npx prisma migrate deploy
   ```

3. **Rollback (if needed)**

   ```
   npx prisma migrate reset
   ```

Flowchart: Migration Lifecycle

Define Schema in Code → Create Migration → Apply to Dev DB

↓   ↓

Commit to Git ← Run in CI/CD → Apply to Prod DB

Best Practices

- Always test migrations locally before applying them in production.

- Use clear migration names (add_user_table, add_index_email).

- Keep backups of production databases before large changes.

10.4 Monitoring, Logging, and Performance Tracking

Why Monitoring is Critical

Aspect	Importance
Error Tracking	Identify and respond to bugs quickly.

Performance	Detect slow APIs, queries, or frontend bottlenecks.
Uptime	Ensure the application remains accessible.
Usage Metrics	Understand user behavior and usage patterns.

Monitoring Stack Options

Tool	Use Case	Hosted Option	Self-Hosted
LogRocket	Frontend monitoring + sessions	✓	✗
Sentry	Error reporting + tracing	✓	✓
Prometheus	Metrics collection	✗	✓
Grafana	Dashboard visualization	✓ (Cloud)	✓

Datadog	All-in-one observability	✓	✗

Step-by-Step: Setting Up Logging and Monitoring

Install a Logger (Node.js Example)

npm install winston

const winston = require('winston');

const logger = winston.createLogger({

  level: 'info',

  transports: [new winston.transports.Console()],

});

logger.info('Server started');

1. **Connect to Sentry**

    npm install @sentry/node

Sentry.init({ dsn: "your-dsn-url" });

2. **Monitor Performance with Prometheus + Grafana**

    ○ Use exporters to expose metrics.

    ○ Set up Grafana dashboard for visual tracking.

Flowchart: Observability Lifecycle

Application Logs → Logger Middleware → Log Aggregator (e.g., Sentry)

↓

Alerts + Dashboards

↓

Developer Action & Fixes

Performance Tracking Checklist

- ✓ Log all incoming API requests with timestamps.

- ✓ Track latency for database queries.

- ✓ Log memory and CPU usage in production.

- ✓ Use uptime checks for critical endpoints.

- ✓ Set alert thresholds for error rates and slow responses.

Key Takeaways

- Migrations ensure consistent database schema changes across environments.

- Logging is essential for debugging and real-time issue resolution.

- Monitoring tools like Sentry and Prometheus help detect and fix problems proactively.

- Combine logs, alerts, and dashboards for full observability.

10.5 Keeping Your AI-Powered App Updated

Why Ongoing Updates Matter

Factor	Reason to Update
AI Model Evolution	LLMs and AI agents improve over time—updating allows you to leverage enhancements.
Security	Patches close vulnerabilities and prevent data breaches.
Feature Expansion	Enables integration of new capabilities and services.

Performance	Updates can optimize speed, resource usage, and user experience.

Types of Updates

Update Type	Description
Model Updates	Improve or replace LLMs and agents with better-performing versions.
Dependency Updates	Refresh libraries, SDKs, and frameworks to latest stable versions.
Infrastructure Changes	Upgrade hosting, containers, or database systems.
Business Logic Changes	Reflect changes in features, policies, or workflows.
UI/UX Enhancements	Improve accessibility, responsiveness, and design clarity.

Flowchart: Update Lifecycle

Identify Needed Updates

↓

Evaluate Risks & Dependencies

↓

Apply Updates in Development

↓

Test in Staging Environment

↓

Deploy to Production

↓

Monitor and Rollback if Needed

Step-by-Step Guide to Updating an AI-Powered App

1. **Monitor Dependencies**

   o Use tools like npm audit, pip list --outdated, or yarn upgrade-interactive.

2. **Check for LLM Improvements**

   o Review the changelogs of the LLM/AI provider (e.g., DeepAgent release notes).

3. **Create a Versioned Backup**

   o   Before applying updates, take a snapshot of the app and database.

4. **Apply Changes Locally**

   o   Update code, models, or packages.

   o   Run unit and integration tests.

5. **Deploy to Staging**

   o   Use a staging environment to simulate production use.

6. **Perform Regression Testing**

   o   Confirm existing functionality is not broken by the update.

7. **Deploy to Production**

   o   Use zero-downtime deployment if possible (e.g., blue-green, rolling updates).

8. **Monitor Logs and Metrics**

   o   Watch error rates, latency, and user engagement metrics for anomalies.

Version Control and Semantic Tagging

Use Semantic Versioning (SemVer) to label changes:

Version Format	Meaning	Example
MAJOR.MINOR.PATCH	Breaking.Feature.Bugfix	2.3.1
1.0.0	Initial Release	
1.1.0	Added new AI integration	
1.1.1	Fixed authentication bug	

Proactive Update Strategies

- **Schedule Monthly Maintenance Windows**

    o Allocate time each month for dependency review and testing.

- **Enable Auto-Update for Non-Critical Packages**

    o Use renovate or dependabot to automatically update minor/patch versions.

- **Stay Informed**

    o Subscribe to newsletters or GitHub repositories for AI tool and framework updates.

Callout: Tip

💡 **Tip**: Always keep your database migrations versioned and in sync with application updates to avoid schema mismatches during deployment.

Key Takeaways

- Regular updates enhance security, performance, and feature richness.

- Semantic versioning and testing prevent disruption during updates.

- Staging environments and monitoring tools reduce risk during deployment.

- Proactive strategies like automated dependency tools streamline the update process.

Chapter 11: Advanced Features and Optimization

11.1 Workflow Optimization Strategies

Why Optimize Workflows?

Goal	Benefit
Reduce Latency	Faster response times improve UX and system efficiency.
Lower Resource Usage	Cuts hosting and compute costs, particularly when using LLMs.
Improve Task Accuracy	Streamlined tasks reduce processing errors or inconsistent behavior.
Enable Scalability	Efficient workflows scale more predictably under load.

Common Workflow Bottlenecks

- Redundant logic across triggers or agents.

- Overuse of synchronous tasks or API calls.

- Poor prompt design causing unpredictable LLM behavior.

- Inefficient loops or polling instead of event-based triggers.

Flowchart: Optimizing a Workflow in DeepAgent

Identify Workflow Bottlenecks

↓

Profile Task Execution Times

↓

Remove Redundant or Sequential Tasks

↓

Convert Synchronous Calls to Async/Queued

↓

Optimize LLM Prompts and Outputs

↓

Retest Workflow for Efficiency

Best Practices for Workflow Optimization

- **Use asynchronous agents** for slow external calls or LLM queries.

- **Group related tasks** into a single reusable module/agent.

- **Use environment-based branching** to avoid executing full workflows in dev/testing.

- **Set intelligent conditions** for branching and early exits.

- **Avoid unnecessary LLM calls**—reuse cached responses or small transformers if available.

Example Table: Optimizing AI Workflow Conditions

Original Pattern	Optimized Pattern	Why It's Better
Run sentiment analysis on all messages	Run only if keyword detected	Reduces LLM usage on irrelevant inputs
Call external API on every submission	Cache results for 1 hour	Lowers load and rate-limiting issues
Loop through DB rows for matching users	Use indexed query with filter	Drastically improves database performance

Key Takeaways

- Optimize workflows by eliminating unnecessary tasks and using async logic.

- Profile slow tasks using logs or timestamps.

- Smart conditions reduce load and improve overall responsiveness.

11.2 Scaling for Traffic and Performance

Scaling Challenges in AI-Powered Apps

Challenge	Cause	Impact
High Latency	LLM response time, cold starts	Poor UX, timeouts
Concurrent User Loads	Many users triggering workflows simultaneously	System crashes or slowdowns
Resource Contention	Memory/CPU limits on containers or shared servers	Throttling or failed executions
Storage and I/O	Large datasets or inefficient queries	Slow database reads/writes

Scaling Approaches

Scaling Type	Description	Example Tooling
Horizontal	Add more containers/instances	Kubernetes, Docker Swarm
Vertical	Upgrade CPU, RAM on existing instance	Cloud instance upgrade
Distributed Queues	Offload long tasks to async queues	Redis Queue, RabbitMQ
Caching	Store frequent responses or data	Redis, Varnish, CDN
Auto-Scaling	Automatically adjust capacity	AWS Lambda, GCP Cloud Run

Step-by-Step Guide: Scaling a DeepAgent App

1. **Profile System Load**

   o Use built-in logs or monitoring tools to analyze resource use.

2. **Enable Asynchronous Execution**

   o Move long-running or LLM-intensive tasks to async workflows or queues.

3. **Use Load Testing Tools**

   o Simulate users with k6, Artillery, or Postman collections.

4. **Optimize Database Performance**

   o Add indexes, normalize/denormalize data, batch queries.

5. **Introduce Caching**

   o Cache API calls, static content, and processed LLM outputs.

6. **Configure Auto-Scaling**

   o Use serverless infrastructure or container orchestrators to scale on demand.

Flowchart: Traffic Scaling Decision

Experiencing Performance Lag?

↓

Yes → Is it CPU/Memory Bound?

↓   ↘

Yes   No

$\downarrow$ $\qquad$ $\downarrow$

Upgrade Instance   Add Load Balancer + Horizontal Scaling

$\downarrow$

Deploy Caching → Setup Monitoring → Optimize DB Queries

Key Takeaways

- Use horizontal and vertical scaling together for optimal performance.

- Async tasks and caching reduce load during peak usage.

- Load test proactively and monitor key performance metrics.

- Choose infrastructure that can scale with minimal manual intervention.

11.3 Implementing Caching, Queues, and Rate Limiting

Caching: Speed Up Repeated Requests

Use Case	Caching Method	Tool Example

API responses	Memory cache	Redis, in-memory store
LLM-generated outputs	Keyed by prompt hash	Redis, SQLite
Frequently read DB results	Query cache	Prisma, Sequelize cache
Static frontend data (e.g., menus)	Local or CDN caching	Browser cache, Vercel Edge

Text-Based Flow: When to Cache

User Makes Request

↓

Is Request Repeated or Predictable?

↓   ↘

Yes   No

↓   ↓

Check Cache   Process as Normal

↓

If Cache Hit → Serve Cached Result

Else → Process & Store in Cache

Queues: Handle Background and Async Tasks

Use queues to **offload resource-intensive or delayed tasks** such as:

- Sending emails or notifications

- Running long LLM tasks

- Batch-processing large datasets

- Handling webhook payloads

Example Task Queue System

Feature	Benefit
Delayed processing	Prevents slow tasks from blocking users
Retry logic	Recovers from transient errors
Parallelism	Multiple workers for faster throughput

Queue Implementation Steps (DeepAgent-Compatible)

1. **Choose a Queue Library** (e.g., BullMQ for Node.js, Celery for Python).

2. **Wrap your async tasks** into job functions (e.g., process_email_job()).

3. **Push jobs to the queue** from your DeepAgent backend logic.

4. **Run workers** separately to process jobs.

5. **Add monitoring** to track queue health and failures.

Rate Limiting: Protect Resources and APIs

Rate limiting prevents **abuse, spamming**, or **unintended loops** in your automation or API use.

Method	Description	Example Limit
IP-based	Max requests per IP in a timeframe	100 reqs/min/IP
User-token-based	Restrict by user auth token	1000 reqs/day
Feature-level	Limit expensive actions like LLM calls	10 reqs/hour

Best Practices

- Use libraries like **express-rate-limit**, **FastAPI-limiter**, or **nginx throttle**.

- Set global and endpoint-specific rules.

- Include proper error codes (e.g., 429 Too Many Requests).

Key Takeaways

- **Cache predictable outputs** to reduce load and speed up UX.

- **Use task queues** to handle delays without blocking workflows.

- **Apply rate limits** to safeguard APIs and control resource usage.

11.4 Custom Prompt Templates and Agent Personalization

Why Customize Prompts?

Goal	Example Outcome
Increase LLM accuracy	More relevant responses with fewer hallucinations
Match app tone and domain	Friendly chatbot for education, formal for legal

Optimize output format	JSON, Markdown, code blocks, etc.
Enable multi-role agents	Use role-specific instructions or constraints

Prompt Template Structure

A good prompt template is:

[Context] + [Instruction] + [Constraints] + [Expected Format]

Example: Structured Prompt for Generating API Docs

You are an API documentation assistant.

Take the following endpoint data and generate markdown-formatted docs.

Only use the fields provided and do not add extra commentary.

Input: { "method": "POST", "endpoint": "/user", "desc": "Create new user" }

Dynamic Prompt Variables

Variable	Source	Example Value

{{user_input}}	Frontend user input	"Generate task list"
{{project_schema}}	From app schema/entity config	JSON schema string
{{session_id}}	Runtime context	"session_abc123"

Agent Personalization Techniques

- **Role-based instructions**:

  - "You are a legal compliance bot. Only answer in legal terms."

- **Tone and language control**:

  - "Write in a casual, friendly tone."

- **Contextual memory** (where supported):

  - Inject previously stored data (e.g., {{last_action_summary}}) into prompts.

Template Best Practices

Practice	Why It Helps
Use placeholders	Avoid hardcoding values

Keep constraints clear	Prevent vague or verbose responses
Test multiple variants	Refine outputs based on feedback
Separate logic from content	Easier to reuse across different use cases

Key Takeaways

- Design reusable prompt templates with placeholders and context.

- Customize prompts to match the agent's role, tone, and task.

- Use personalization to increase reliability, format consistency, and relevance.

11.5 Combining DeepAgent with Other AI Tools (e.g., LangChain, AutoGen)

Why Combine DeepAgent with Other Tools?

Tool	What It Adds to DeepAgent

LangChain	LLM orchestration, tool chaining, memory injection
AutoGen	Multi-agent collaboration, planning, role separation
LlamaIndex	Indexing documents and data for prompt retrieval

Integration Flow Example: DeepAgent + LangChain

User Input

↓

DeepAgent Initial Prompt Handling

↓

LangChain Pipeline

- Adds tools (SQL, browser, docs)

- Injects context/memory

- Formats response

↓

Final Output to User

Code Snippet: Wrapping DeepAgent Output with LangChain

```python
from langchain.agents import initialize_agent, Tool

from langchain.llms import OpenAI

from deepagent_sdk import run_deepagent_prompt


def deepagent_tool_fn(input):

    return run_deepagent_prompt(input)


tools = [Tool(name="DeepAgentRunner", func=deepagent_tool_fn, description="Runs prompts using DeepAgent")]


llm = OpenAI(temperature=0)

agent = initialize_agent(tools, llm, agent_type="zero-shot-react-description")


response = agent.run("Generate a CRUD API for a blog platform.")
```

Use Cases for LangChain + DeepAgent

- Pre-processing: Use LangChain to fetch external data before sending to DeepAgent.

- Post-processing: Format or re-structure DeepAgent's output (e.g., parse code, add metadata).

- Dynamic tool invocation: Automatically call different services based on the prompt.

Using AutoGen with DeepAgent

AutoGen enables complex workflows with **multiple cooperating agents**, each with specialized roles.

Example Multi-Agent Setup

Agent Name	Role	Integration with DeepAgent
PlannerAgent	Plans features	Sends feature plan prompt to DeepAgent
CodeAgent	Writes code	Uses DeepAgent's backend generator
QA Agent	Reviews and tests output	Feeds DeepAgent output for review

Best Practices

- Clearly define roles and interfaces between agents.

- Use intermediate memory to track state between prompts.

- Ensure DeepAgent outputs are clean and structured for chaining.

Key Takeaways

- LangChain enhances DeepAgent with tools, memory, and chaining.

- AutoGen supports structured multi-agent development workflows.

- These tools make DeepAgent suitable for **complex orchestration scenarios**.

11.6 AI Model Customization and Fine-Tuning: Tailoring DeepAgent for Your Needs

Objective

Three Levels of Customization

Level	Description	Complexity

Prompt Design	Modify instructions, tone, format	Low
Contextual Memory	Inject user/app-specific context	Medium
Fine-Tuning Models	Retrain model weights with custom data	High

Level 1: Prompt Design

We covered prompt templating earlier. You can further personalize with:

- Business terminology

- Expected coding patterns (e.g., REST over GraphQL)

- Format preferences (e.g., camelCase for fields)

Example: Custom Prompt for Invoice App

You are a backend engineer for a finance app.

Use camelCase for field names. Generate Node.js Express routes.

Use MongoDB with Mongoose. Validate currency formats in inputs.

Level 2: Contextual Memory and Profiles

Add persistent or session-based memory to improve consistency.

Feature	How to Implement
Session history	Store recent prompts/responses in cache
User profile injection	Pass user preferences (tech stack, tone)
App schema injection	Auto-feed entity structures into prompts

Level 3: Fine-Tuning the LLM

If DeepAgent supports backend customization or private model hosting, consider training on your specific data.

Fine-Tuning Workflow Overview

Collect Domain Data (Code, Docs, Logs)

↓

Clean and Format Data into Prompt/Response Pairs

↓

Use LLM APIs (e.g., OpenAI fine-tuning endpoint)

↓

Deploy Fine-Tuned Model or Adapter (LoRA, PEFT)

When to Fine-Tune

- Repetitive or specialized tasks

- Domain jargon (legal, healthcare, etc.)

- Custom logic patterns (e.g., fintech workflows)

Tips for Effective Fine-Tuning

- Use **few-shot examples** before jumping to full fine-tuning.

- Keep prompts deterministic (low temperature).

- Validate model changes on real-world tasks.

Key Takeaways

- Start with prompt and context customization before fine-tuning.

- Use user profiles and app schemas to tailor outputs.

- Fine-tuning is powerful but requires clean data and careful planning.

Chapter 12: Real-World Projects and Final Thoughts

12.1 AI-Powered CRM (Customer Relationship Management System)

Features Overview

Step-by-Step Guide

1. **Requirements Gathering**

   Use DeepAgent to collect input like:

   - "Build a CRM with contact management, follow-up automation, and a dashboard."

2. **Data Model Generation**

   - Entities: Contact, Interaction, Reminder, PipelineStage

   - Relationships: One-to-many (Contact → Interactions)

ERD Sample (Text-Based)

Contact ———< Interaction

```
|
└───< Reminder

|
└───< PipelineStage
```

3. **Backend Generation**

   - Use DeepAgent to auto-generate CRUD APIs.

   - Add AI agents to suggest follow-up dates based on last interaction.

4. **Frontend Components**

   - Contact Table with filters

   - Reminder Card View

   - Lead Funnel Chart

5. **AI Workflow Example**

   - Input: "Schedule next meeting with John Doe"

   - Output: Adds reminder, updates last interaction, drafts email

---

AI Agent Tip

Add an agent that:

- Summarizes recent interactions

- Drafts follow-up messages

- Prioritizes leads based on AI-scored engagement

12.2 Inventory Management System

Features Overview

Feature	Description
Product Catalog	Manage product data including SKUs, categories, and pricing
Stock Management	Track inventory levels, reorder alerts
Supplier Management	Store vendor information, purchase history
Order Processing	Manage restocking, invoices, and shipment tracking
Reporting Dashboard	View low-stock items, sales trends, and supplier KPIs

Step-by-Step Guide

1. **Requirement Prompt**

   ○ "Create an inventory system with product tracking, stock alerts, and supplier management."

2. **Data Model Summary**

Entity	Attributes
Product	SKU, name, quantity, price, category
Supplier	Name, contact info, order history
Order	Product ID, quantity, supplier, status

Entity Relationships

Product ———< Order >——— Supplier

3. **Backend Generation with DeepAgent**

   ○ Use prompt engineering to generate routes like:

- POST /products

- GET /inventory/low-stock

- POST /orders

4. **Frontend Suggestions**

   - Table for products with editable quantities

   - Form to add new suppliers

   - Chart for reorder frequency

5. **Automation Ideas**

   - Automatically generate restock orders when quantity < threshold

   - Alert via Slack/email using webhook

AI Workflow Example

- Input: "Check which products need restocking."

- Output: List of SKUs + supplier recommendations + auto-generated order draft.

Key Takeaways from These Projects

Concept	Demonstrated In
Prompt engineering	Both CRM and Inventory use cases
AI workflow integration	Automated reminders, reorder logic
Schema + ERD design	Text-based planning with DeepAgent
Real-time decision making	AI scoring, inventory predictions

12.3 Customer Support Chatbot with Database Logging

Features Overview

Feature	Description
AI-Powered Chatbot	Interact with customers using NLP and machine learning

Query Logging	Log all customer queries and chatbot responses
Ticket Management	Auto-generate support tickets for unresolved queries
Automated Issue Resolution	Provide automated troubleshooting and resolution tips
Chat History	Store chat logs for future reference

Step-by-Step Guide

1. **Requirement Gathering**

   Use DeepAgent to prompt:

   - "Create a customer support chatbot that logs interactions, generates tickets, and provides automated responses."

2. **Database Schema Design**

Entity	Attributes
Customer	Name, email, contact details

ChatSession	Customer ID, timestamp, status
Ticket	Chat session ID, issue description
Resolution	Ticket ID, resolution status

ERD Sample (Text-Based)

Customer ——< ChatSession ——< Ticket

                └——< Resolution

3. **Backend API Generation**

   o Generate APIs such as:

   ■ POST /chatbot/query

   ■ GET /chat/history

   ■ POST /ticket/new

4. **AI Workflow Integration**

   o For unresolved issues, the chatbot creates a ticket and escalates it.

   o AI models provide automated responses based on a pre-trained knowledge base.

5. **Frontend Design Suggestions**

- Chat interface with message bubbles

- View chat history and active tickets

- Automated responses in the chatbot window

AI Workflow Example

- **Input**: "I can't login to my account."

- **Output**: Chatbot provides troubleshooting steps and logs the query.

- **If unresolved**: "Creating support ticket...," then generates a ticket in the database.

AI Agent Tip

Add an agent that:

- Suggests FAQs for common issues

- Tracks ticket status and reminds the support team of pending tickets

---

12.4 E-commerce Backend with Smart Inventory Sync

Features Overview

Feature	Description
Product Catalog	Manage product details, pricing, and descriptions
Order Management	Track orders from initiation to fulfillment
Payment Processing	Integrate with payment gateways for secure transactions
Inventory Sync	Automatically update inventory levels across platforms
Reporting and Analytics	Generate sales reports, trends, and inventory forecasts

Step-by-Step Guide

1. **Requirement Prompt**

- "Build an e-commerce backend that supports product management, order processing, and syncs inventory across multiple platforms."

2. **Data Model Design**

Entity	Attributes
Product	SKU, name, price, stock level, description
Order	Order ID, product IDs, quantity, status
Payment	Order ID, payment status, amount
Inventory	Product ID, stock level, last updated

Entity Relationships

```
Product ——< Order >—— Payment

   |          |

   └——< Inventory └——< Transaction
```

3. **Backend API Generation**

- Auto-generate APIs such as:

- POST /orders

- GET /products

- GET /inventory/sync

4. **AI Workflow Integration**

   - Sync inventory levels with other platforms (e.g., marketplaces like Amazon, Shopify).

   - Provide restock suggestions based on AI-driven demand predictions.

   - Create automated promotions based on sales trends.

5. **Frontend Design Suggestions**

   - Product listing with dynamic stock updates

   - Order tracking interface

   - Integration with a payment system for secure checkout

AI Workflow Example

- **Input**: "Sync inventory across all platforms."

- **Output**: Inventory levels updated across the e-commerce website, mobile app, and third-party marketplaces.

AI Agent Tip

Implement an AI agent that:

- Sends alerts when stock is low across multiple platforms.

- Suggests dynamic pricing based on inventory levels and market demand.

Key Takeaways from These Projects

Concept	Demonstrated In
AI-powered customer service	Both chatbot interaction and ticket generation
Real-time inventory management	Syncing inventory across different platforms
Automated workflows	Creating tickets, syncing inventory, processing payments

12.5 Lead Generation App with Automated Emailing

Features Overview

Feature	Description
Lead Capture Form	Collect contact information (name, email, company, etc.)
Lead Qualification	Use AI to score and qualify leads based on criteria
Automated Email Follow-up	Send personalized follow-up emails at predefined intervals
CRM Integration	Sync leads with CRM systems like Salesforce, HubSpot, etc.
Reporting and Analytics	Track lead generation statistics, email open rates, etc.

Step-by-Step Guide

1. **Requirement Gathering Prompt**

- "Create a lead generation app that captures leads, qualifies them, and sends automated emails based on AI-driven behavior analysis."

2. Database Schema Design

Entity	Attributes
Lead	Name, email, company, qualification score, date
EmailCampaign	Lead ID, subject, body, sent status, timestamp
Interaction	Lead ID, email open status, click-through rate

Entity Relationships

Lead ——< EmailCampaign

└——< Interaction

3. Backend API Generation

- Auto-generate APIs such as:

  - POST /leads

- GET /leads/{id}

- POST /emails/send

- Use AI prompts to generate personalized email templates based on lead data.

4. **Lead Qualification with AI**

   - Train an AI model to score leads based on attributes like:

     - Engagement level

     - Company size

     - Industry

     - Lead source

5. **Email Template Generation**

   - Use DeepAgent to generate personalized email content:

     - "Hi {{first_name}}, based on your interest in {{product}}, I wanted to share..."

   - Automate the follow-up sequence (e.g., Day 1: Initial contact, Day 3: Reminder, Day 7: Final follow-up).

6. **AI-Driven Email Campaign Management**

   - Track email opens and click-through rates.

- AI adjusts follow-up strategy based on interaction data (e.g., if a lead clicks but doesn't respond, trigger a more targeted email).

7. **CRM Integration**

   - Auto-sync new leads with your CRM system.

   - Use DeepAgent to create an integration flow for platforms like Salesforce or HubSpot.

AI Workflow Example

- **Input**: "Lead submitted through web form."

- **Output**:

   - AI qualifies the lead based on predefined criteria.

   - A personalized email is sent to the lead with the appropriate follow-up plan.

   - Email status is tracked, and the system updates the lead's qualification score.

AI Agent Tip

- Implement an AI agent that:

   - Scores leads in real-time based on their behavior and engagement with your website or marketing materials.

- Optimizes email sending times based on lead activity (e.g., sending emails when leads are most likely to engage).

Frontend Design Suggestions

1. **Lead Capture Form**

   - Simple, user-friendly form to collect contact details.

   - Show lead qualification status (e.g., "Qualified," "Unqualified").

2. **Lead Dashboard**

   - Display a list of captured leads with basic info (name, email, score).

   - Show email campaign history and interaction stats.

3. **Email Campaign Tracker**

   - Display emails sent, open rates, and next follow-up dates.

   - Allow users to manually adjust email templates or automation settings.

AI Workflow Example for Email Automation

1. **Input:** "New lead entered via form."

2. **AI Action:**

- AI scores the lead.

- Personalized email is generated and sent.

- Follow-up emails are scheduled based on lead interaction.

3. **If Lead Opens Email**:

   - AI tracks open rates, adjusting the email flow based on engagement.

   - If no response is received after a second email, the system automatically escalates the lead to a sales team.

Key Takeaways from This Project

Concept	Demonstrated In
Automated Lead Capture	Using forms to collect lead information
AI-Driven Lead Qualification	AI scoring and segmenting leads based on criteria
Email Automation	Sending personalized emails and automating follow-ups
CRM Integration	Syncing leads with CRM systems like HubSpot or Salesforce

Next Steps

- **Deploy the Lead Generation App** using cloud hosting (e.g., AWS, Vercel).

- **Monitor and analyze** the effectiveness of email campaigns.

- **Optimize lead qualification** over time using data-driven insights.

This project is an excellent example of how DeepAgent can automate and optimize business processes, from lead capture to follow-up emails, all using AI-powered automation. It also highlights the versatility of DeepAgent in integrating with existing tools and services like CRMs, email platforms, and analytics.

Chapter 13: Security, Ethics, and Responsible AI Development

13.1 Securing APIs, Databases, and User Accounts

In this section, we will cover the essential practices and principles for securing your AI-powered application, focusing on APIs, databases, and user accounts.

Securing APIs

APIs serve as the backbone for communication between your AI-powered app and external services or other components of your system. Securing APIs is critical to prevent unauthorized access and potential misuse of your app's data.

Best Practices for API Security:

Practice	Description
Use API Keys	Secure each API endpoint by requiring a valid API key to access the service.
Rate Limiting	Prevent API abuse by limiting the number of requests per user per time period.
OAuth 2.0 Authentication	Use OAuth for secure, token-based user authentication and authorization.

Encryption (HTTPS)	Always encrypt data in transit by using HTTPS to prevent interception.
Input Validation	Validate user inputs to prevent SQL injection and other attacks.
API Gateway	Use an API gateway to add an extra layer of security for managing traffic and implementing security policies.

Example:

For securing an API endpoint that interacts with your database, you can implement the following logic:

1. **Require Authentication**: Use OAuth tokens or API keys for authentication.

2. **Secure Data Transmission**: Ensure that data is transmitted over HTTPS.

3. **Input Sanitization**: Validate and sanitize inputs to prevent malicious data injections.

Securing Databases

Databases often store sensitive user data, making them a prime target for attackers. Securing your database is crucial for protecting both personal data and business-critical information.

Best Practices for Database Security:

Practice	Description
Encryption at Rest	Encrypt sensitive data stored in the database to prevent unauthorized access.
Access Control	Use role-based access control (RBAC) to ensure users can only access their data.
Use Strong Passwords	Require strong passwords for all database user accounts.
Database Backups	Regularly back up your database and store backups securely.
Regular Updates	Keep your database software up to date to patch vulnerabilities.
SQL Injection Protection	Use parameterized queries and ORM libraries to prevent SQL injection attacks.

Example:

You can use a tool like **SQLAlchemy** with Python to implement ORM-based queries, which automatically protect against SQL injection by using parameterized queries.

```
# Example of a parameterized query using SQLAlchemy

session.query(User).filter(User.email == :email).params(email="user@example.com").first()
```

Securing User Accounts

Ensuring the security of user accounts is paramount, especially when dealing with sensitive personal information. Here are key practices to protect user accounts.

Best Practices for User Account Security:

Practice	Description
Password Hashing	Use strong hashing algorithms (e.g., bcrypt, Argon2) to store passwords securely.
Multi-Factor Authentication (MFA)	Implement MFA to require additional verification (e.g., email or SMS code) after password entry.
Session Management	Properly manage sessions by using secure cookies and implementing session expiration.
User Input Sanitization	Protect against XSS and other attacks by sanitizing user input.
Password Strength Enforcement	Enforce minimum password length and complexity requirements.

Example:

Using **bcrypt** for password hashing in Python:

```python
import bcrypt


# Hash a password

hashed_password = bcrypt.hashpw(password.encode('utf-8'), bcrypt.gensalt())


# Verify a password

if bcrypt.checkpw(password.encode('utf-8'), hashed_password):

    print("Password match!")

else:

    print("Incorrect password.")
```

13.2 Avoiding Prompt Injection and AI Misuse

AI systems like DeepAgent generate outputs based on prompts, but they are vulnerable to misuse, particularly prompt injection. Prompt injection occurs when an attacker manipulates the input provided to the AI to produce unintended or malicious outputs.

What is Prompt Injection?

Prompt injection refers to feeding malicious or misleading data to an AI system in a way that causes it to generate harmful or unintended responses. This can be particularly problematic when the AI is generating dynamic content, making decisions, or interacting with users.

Examples of Prompt Injection:

1. **Injection into AI's prompt**: Manipulating user input or API calls to change the behavior of AI-generated content.

2. **Bypassing User Input Validation**: Passing malicious commands or queries via the input fields to alter how the AI interprets and processes data.

Best Practices to Avoid Prompt Injection

Practice	Description
Input Validation	Validate and sanitize all inputs to prevent manipulation.
Limit AI Output Scope	Restrict the AI's response domain, especially when generating content for critical tasks (e.g., transactions, sensitive data).
Monitor Outputs	Continuously monitor AI outputs for unusual or suspicious responses.
Use AI Output Filters	Use filters to detect and block harmful content or malicious instructions generated by the AI.
Contextualize Prompts	Avoid giving the AI too much flexibility in interpreting user inputs. Limit the scope of the prompt to the intended task.

Example:

If you're building a chatbot, ensure that the prompts are clearly scoped to avoid unexpected behavior from the AI.

```
prompt = "Answer only questions about our products. Do not provide advice on unrelated topics."

response = deepagent.generate(prompt)
```

Ethical Considerations and Responsible AI

It's essential to develop AI applications responsibly, ensuring that AI models do not perpetuate harm, biases, or unethical behavior.

Ethical AI Development Practices:

Practice	Description
Bias Mitigation	Actively work to reduce biases in the data used to train AI models.
Transparency	Provide clear documentation on how AI models work and what data they are trained on.
Data Privacy	Ensure that AI models comply with data privacy regulations (e.g., GDPR).

Accountability	Implement systems to track and audit AI decisions, ensuring accountability for automated actions.
Inclusive AI	Develop AI solutions that are inclusive and accessible to all users, regardless of their background or identity.

Key Takeaways from This Chapter

Concept	Explanation
API Security	Use best practices like OAuth, rate limiting, and input validation to secure your APIs.
Database Security	Encrypt sensitive data and ensure only authorized access to databases.
User Account Security	Use password hashing, MFA, and secure session management to protect user accounts.
Prompt Injection Prevention	Validate inputs and limit AI output scope to prevent prompt manipulation.

Ethical AI Development	Work to reduce bias, ensure transparency, and promote inclusivity in AI applications.

Next Steps

- **Review and implement** these security measures as part of your AI-powered application development process.

- **Integrate ethical guidelines** into your AI development workflow to ensure your app remains fair, transparent, and responsible.

- **Test for vulnerabilities** regularly and stay updated on new AI security best practices to protect your users and data.

13.3 Ethical AI Usage in Applications

Ethical use of AI in applications is critical to building trust, ensuring user safety, and maintaining social responsibility. As AI systems like DeepAgent become more capable, developers must proactively integrate ethical principles into their design, deployment, and ongoing maintenance.

Why Ethical AI Usage Matters

AI systems have the power to:

- Influence decisions (e.g., financial, legal, medical)

- Automate communication (e.g., chatbots, assistants)

- Affect user behavior and perceptions

If not used ethically, AI can amplify harm—either through negligence (e.g., privacy violations) or active misuse (e.g., deceptive automation).

Key Principles of Ethical AI Usage

Principle	Description
Transparency	Clearly communicate when and how AI is used in the application.
Fairness	Ensure the system does not discriminate based on race, gender, religion, etc.
Accountability	Developers must be accountable for the AI's decisions and behavior.
Privacy Protection	Do not collect or use user data beyond what is necessary.
Explainability	Provide users with explanations of how AI decisions are made when possible.
Consent	Obtain informed consent for collecting data or using AI-generated results.

Examples of Ethical Use Scenarios

Use Case	Ethical Approach
AI-Powered Hiring Tool	Ensure the model is trained on unbiased data and explain decision rationale.
Health Advice Chatbot	Include disclaimers; redirect users to certified professionals.
E-commerce Recommendation AI	Let users know recommendations are AI-generated and based on tracked behavior.

Ethical Flags to Avoid

- Using AI to impersonate humans without disclosure

- Auto-approving sensitive decisions (e.g., loans, bans) without human review

- Selling user data inferred via AI without explicit consent

Tip

Always conduct an **AI Ethics Impact Assessment** before launching your app to identify and mitigate risks early.

13.4 Bias Mitigation and Model Limitations

AI models are only as good as the data they are trained on. When biases exist in the training data, they are often reflected and amplified in the model's outputs. This creates fairness risks—especially in applications that affect people's lives.

Types of Bias in AI Systems

Type of Bias	Description
Historical Bias	Bias present in the original data due to societal inequalities.
Sampling Bias	Occurs when training data doesn't represent the entire user population.
Label Bias	Introduced by subjective or inconsistent labeling practices.
Measurement Bias	Arises from how inputs and outcomes are quantified (e.g., flawed metrics).

Techniques for Mitigating Bias

Method	Description
Diverse Training Data	Use representative data covering various demographics and contexts.
Bias Audits	Regularly test the model for unequal performance across groups.
Model Explainability	Use tools like SHAP or LIME to understand how models reach decisions.
Human-in-the-Loop	Keep a human review stage in high-risk decision processes.
Regular Retraining	Update models as new, less biased data becomes available.

Recognizing and Communicating Model Limitations

AI models have **inherent limitations**—they can hallucinate, misinterpret intent, or fail in edge cases. It's critical to communicate these limitations to users clearly.

Best Practices:

- Display warnings or disclaimers where AI decisions affect user outcomes.

- Document use cases where the AI is not recommended.

- Provide fallback options (e.g., human support).

Example Warning for Users

"This response is AI-generated based on available data. It may not always be accurate. Please verify with a human representative for critical actions."

Summary Table

Topic	Key Takeaway
Ethical AI Usage	Design AI apps transparently, fairly, and with clear accountability.
Bias Mitigation	Identify, test, and reduce bias through better data and oversight.
Model Limitations	Clearly communicate what the AI can and cannot do.
Trust through Design	Include disclaimers, opt-outs, and human review in sensitive scenarios.

Key Takeaways

- **Ethics is not optional**: Responsible AI usage should be part of your core development cycle, not an afterthought.

- **Bias can be hidden**: Just because a model performs well overall doesn't mean it performs fairly for everyone.

- **Be transparent**: Let users know how AI is used and where its limits lie.

13.5 Privacy Compliance: GDPR, CCPA, and More

As AI-powered applications increasingly handle sensitive user data, compliance with data protection laws becomes a legal and ethical obligation. Regulations such as the **General Data Protection Regulation (GDPR)** in the EU and the **California Consumer Privacy Act (CCPA)** in the US establish strict rules on how personal data is collected, stored, and used.

This section will help you understand the fundamentals of privacy compliance when building apps with DeepAgent.

Overview of Major Privacy Regulations

Regulation	Region	Key Principles
GDPR (General Data Protection Regulation)	European Union	Lawful, fair, and transparent processing; data minimization; accountability;

		user rights (e.g., access, erasure)
CCPA (California Consumer Privacy Act)	California, USA	Right to know, right to delete, right to opt-out of data sales, non-discrimination
HIPAA (Health Insurance Portability and Accountability Act)	USA	Applies to healthcare data; requires security, privacy, and breach notifications
PIPEDA (Personal Information Protection and Electronic Documents Act)	Canada	Consent, accountability, limited collection, individual access
LGPD (Lei Geral de Proteção de Dados)	Brazil	Similar to GDPR; includes principles of purpose, adequacy, and necessity

Key Compliance Areas for AI-Powered Applications

1. Data Collection and Consent

- Collect only the data needed for the app to function (data minimization).

- Explicitly inform users how their data will be used.

- Provide opt-in/opt-out mechanisms, especially for tracking or data sharing.

Tip: Use AI-generated prompts from DeepAgent to automatically create privacy policy templates based on your app's features.

---

2. User Rights Management

Implement systems to handle:

- **Data access requests**: Users should be able to view their stored data.

- **Data deletion**: Users can request to delete their data ("right to be forgotten").

- **Data portability**: Users can request their data in a readable format.

Example Flowchart:

[User Request] → [Verify Identity] → [Fetch Data] → [Respond/Delete/Export]

---

3. Data Storage and Security

- Encrypt data at rest and in transit.

- Store data in compliant regions (e.g., EU data should not leave the EU unless allowed).

- Use environment variables and secrets management to avoid exposing credentials in code.

Best Practices:

- Use GDPR/CCPA-compliant database hosting providers.

- Conduct regular security audits and penetration tests.

4. AI-Specific Privacy Concerns

Concern	Mitigation
AI-generated logs may store personal data	Sanitize logs and remove sensitive inputs
Models may memorize personal information	Use differential privacy or fine-tuning controls
Prompts can inadvertently extract private data	Apply strict input validation and content filtering

Example: GDPR-Compliant Workflow for a DeepAgent App

[User signs up]

↓

[Consent captured via checkbox + privacy policy link]

↓

[Data stored in encrypted DB, location EU]

↓

[User requests data deletion]

[Admin triggers DeepAgent prompt to remove all associated records]

Checklist: Building a Privacy-Compliant AI App

Requirement	Completed?
Clear, accessible privacy policy	☐
Consent management UI	☐
Data encryption in transit and at rest	☐
Delete/export user data on request	☐
Minimal and purpose-specific data collection	☐
Logging system avoids personal data	☐
Geo-specific data residency compliance	☐

Key Takeaways

- **Privacy laws are not optional**—non-compliance can lead to heavy penalties and reputational damage.

- **DeepAgent apps must include mechanisms for consent, access, and deletion** to meet GDPR and CCPA standards.

- **Minimize risk** by collecting less data, securing it properly, and responding promptly to user requests.

Chapter 14: The Future of AI in App Development

14.1 The Next Generation of Autonomous Agents

The landscape of software development is rapidly transforming due to the rise of **autonomous AI agents**—self-directed, intelligent systems capable of planning, reasoning, and executing tasks with minimal human input. These agents move beyond simple automation and begin to **simulate cognitive behavior**, acting like junior developers or digital project managers within your app development workflow.

Key Characteristics of Next-Gen Agents

Feature	Description
Goal-Oriented	They work toward defined objectives rather than single commands.
Memory-Driven	Agents retain state and learn from past interactions.
Adaptive Planning	They can adjust steps based on obstacles or changing requirements.
Autonomy	They act without continuous human prompts.

Tool Use	Capable of invoking APIs, writing code, querying databases, and managing workflows.

Comparison Table: Traditional Automation vs. Autonomous Agents

Aspect	Traditional Automation	Autonomous AI Agents
Initiation	Requires explicit commands	Can self-initiate actions
Flexibility	Limited, rule-based	Highly adaptable
Task Scope	Single-task focused	Multi-step, goal-oriented
Learning	Static scripts	Learns from environment and outcomes

Use Cases for Next-Gen Agents

- Auto-generating full-stack applications based on natural language specs.

- Monitoring production systems and refactoring underperforming components.

- Performing security audits or optimizing code during runtime.

- Managing CI/CD pipelines autonomously.

Tip: DeepAgent's future roadmap includes supporting persistent, memory-aware agents that evolve their behavior over time, offering real-time collaboration on long-term projects.

14.2 Multi-Agent Collaboration and Task Delegation

As systems become more complex, the solution isn't a more powerful single agent—but **multiple specialized agents** that work together. This approach, called **multi-agent collaboration**, brings modularity, speed, and improved reliability to AI-assisted development.

What Are Multi-Agent Systems (MAS)?

MAS are frameworks where several AI agents collaborate—communicating and delegating tasks—to complete complex goals that exceed the capabilities of a single agent.

Advantages of Multi-Agent Collaboration

Benefit	Explanation
Parallel Processing	Agents execute tasks simultaneously, reducing total time.
Division of Labor	Each agent focuses on its area of expertise (e.g., UI, backend, logic).
Fault Tolerance	Failure in one agent doesn't disrupt the entire process.
Reusable Agents	Modular agents can be reused across multiple projects.

Continuous Feedback	Agents can validate and refine each other's outputs.

DeepAgent and Agent Collaboration

DeepAgent supports this model by:

- Assigning different prompts to different agents.

- Managing context between agents using shared memory or structured prompts.

- Offering users control over agent workflows and task priority.

Sample Agent Roles in DeepAgent

Agent	Function
UI Agent	Builds responsive interfaces using frameworks like React.
Data Agent	Designs database schema and relationships.
Backend Agent	Generates API endpoints and core logic.
Workflow Agent	Automates scheduling, triggers, and integrations.

Test Agent	Performs unit testing and catches logic flaws.

Flowchart: Collaborative Agent Workflow

[User Input: "Build Inventory Management App"]

↓

[Coordinator Agent]

↓

```
┌─────────┬─────────┬─────────┬─────────┐
```

↓   ↓   ↓   ↓

[UI Agent] [Backend Agent] [Data Agent] [Workflow Agent]

↓   ↓   ↓   ↓

[Generate UI] [Create APIs] [Design Schema] [Set Up Triggers]

↓   ↓   ↓   ↓

→→→ [Test Agent] ←←←

↓

[Final Application]

Best Practices for Multi-Agent Development

- **Clearly Define Agent Roles** to avoid overlaps and confusion.

- **Use Shared Context Buffers** for consistent information exchange.

- **Prioritize Inter-Agent Feedback Loops** for quality control.

- **Enable Human-in-the-Loop Overrides** where necessary.

✅ **Note:** You can configure agent interactions in DeepAgent using structured prompts like:

"Let the Backend Agent wait for schema generation from the Data Agent before building endpoints."

Key Takeaways

- The future of AI development is driven by autonomous and collaborative agents.

- Next-gen agents work toward goals, learn continuously, and interact with multiple systems.

- Multi-agent setups improve speed, scalability, and reliability by dividing complex workflows.

- DeepAgent is built to support both individual and collaborative AI agents.

14.3 AGI, LLM APIs, and Beyond

The world of AI agents is evolving rapidly, and the horizon includes breakthroughs like **Artificial General Intelligence (AGI)**, smarter **LLM APIs**, and increasingly autonomous platforms. These advancements will redefine what it means to "develop software"—shifting from manual coding to **co-developing** with intelligent machines.

From LLMs to AGI: What's Changing?

Term	Definition
LLM (Large Language Model)	A model trained on vast text corpora to generate human-like text and code.
LLM APIs	Interfaces (e.g., OpenAI, Anthropic, Mistral) allowing developers to integrate LLM capabilities into apps.
AGI (Artificial General Intelligence)	A system capable of reasoning, learning, and performing any intellectual task a human can.

Key Differences Between LLMs and AGI

Criteria	LLM	AGI (Futuristic)
Domain Knowledge	Narrow to general, text-focused	Multidisciplinary and adaptable

Task Autonomy	Needs prompts and boundaries	Operates with long-term goals
Context Retention	Limited memory scope	Persistent, long-term memory
Reasoning	Pattern-based inference	Causal, abstract reasoning

The Future of LLM APIs

As APIs evolve, we can expect:

- **Longer context windows** (e.g., 1M+ tokens)

- **Multimodal capabilities** (text, image, audio, video)

- **Fine-tuned agents-as-a-service** for business-specific logic

- **Persistent memory layers** via tools like vector stores or agent memories

- **Real-time feedback and on-the-fly learning**

💡 **Example:** Instead of writing code, a developer might say:
"Create a cross-platform mobile app that tracks fitness habits and integrates with Apple Health," and the agent will handle planning, coding, and deployment.

Beyond Tools: AI as a Collaborator

Soon, agents will:

- Participate in design discussions

- Review PRs with intelligent context

- Perform A/B testing automatically

- Refactor legacy systems based on usage analytics

This will **reshape the role of the developer**, blending human creativity with machine precision.

14.4 Career Paths for Developers in the AI-Agent Era

As the software landscape evolves, so do developer career opportunities. Rather than making developers obsolete, AI agents **expand the demand** for new skills, roles, and specializations.

Emerging Roles in AI-Powered Development

Role	Description
Prompt Engineer	Crafts effective prompts and workflows for LLMs and agents.
AI Systems Integrator	Combines AI models, databases, APIs, and UI layers into cohesive apps.

Agent Orchestrator	Designs and manages multi-agent systems, workflows, and communication.
AI UX Designer	Builds intuitive interfaces for interacting with intelligent systems.
AI Product Manager	Oversees AI-first product design, testing, and iteration cycles.

Skillsets to Prioritize

Area	Why It Matters
Prompt Engineering	High ROI in agent output quality.
LLM APIs & SDKs	Core tools for integrating AI.
Architecture Design	Required for multi-agent systems.
Ethical AI Principles	Ensures trust, safety, and compliance.
Human-AI Collaboration Models	Helps design effective co-working interfaces.

Traditional Dev Roles Are Evolving, Not Disappearing

Then (2020s)	Now & Future (2030s)
Full-stack Developer	Agent-enhanced System Builder
QA Engineer	AI Feedback Loop Designer
DevOps Engineer	AI Deployment & Monitoring Lead
Data Analyst	LLM-Driven Insight Specialist

⚠️ **Important**: The future will reward **hybrid talent**—those who understand both classical software and AI-based systems.

Key Takeaways

- The rise of AGI and evolving LLM APIs will shift software development toward intelligent co-creation.

- Developers can future-proof their careers by learning AI integration, prompt engineering, and orchestration.

- AI will not eliminate developers—it will elevate them into higher-level, strategic roles.

- Embracing this transformation opens new frontiers in innovation, design, and collaboration.

14.5 Final Thoughts and Encouragement

As we reach the end of this journey through **AI-powered application development**, it's important to pause and reflect on the **transformational power** at your fingertips.

From Developer to AI Co-Creator

You are no longer just writing code line by line. You're:

- **Designing conversations with AI agents**

- **Orchestrating intelligent workflows**

- **Solving problems at a system level**, not just syntax level

This is more than a shift in tooling—it's a **redefinition of how software is imagined and created**.

💬 *"You're no longer limited by what you can code, but by what you can describe."*

You're Ready for the Next Era

By completing this book, you've gained:

- A strong foundation in **agent-based development**

- Practical skills in **using DeepAgent** to plan, build, and launch applications

- The ability to **integrate LLMs, APIs, databases, and automation workflows**

- Awareness of the **ethical, scalable, and future-ready aspects** of AI app development

---

Stay Curious, Keep Exploring

The tools will evolve. The agents will get smarter. The ecosystems will shift. But the core mindset—**curiosity, creativity, and critical thinking**—will always be your greatest asset.

Tips for Continued Growth:

- Join communities (e.g., Discord, GitHub, forums) focused on AI agents

- Contribute to open-source projects using tools like DeepAgent or LangChain

- Follow updates in LLM APIs, new frameworks, and emerging research

- Build projects. Iterate. Experiment.

☐ The best way to learn AI development is to **build with AI, alongside AI.**

A Word of Encouragement

Don't worry if you're not an AI expert yet. No one starts as an expert.

The most impactful developers in the AI-agent era will not be the ones with the fanciest credentials—but the ones who:

- **Start building early**

- **Learn through doing**

- **Stay humble and adaptable**

You've already taken the most important step—**starting the journey**.

Final Call to Action

Go build your first AI-powered database app with DeepAgent.

Then build your second. Then help someone else do the same.

Because the future of software is not built **by AI alone**, but by **humans and AI working together**—and you're now part of that future.

Final Summary Table

You've Learned How To:
Use DeepAgent to build full-stack database apps
Structure scalable data models and workflows
Generate code, UIs, APIs, and logic using AI
Integrate with external tools and automate processes

Test, debug, deploy, and maintain AI-built software
Apply best practices in security, ethics, and AI usage
Prepare for a career in the AI-agent era

Appendices

Appendix A: DeepAgent Prompt Templates

A.1 – Data Model Generation

Prompt:

"Create a relational database schema for a [business type]. Include tables, field types, and relationships. Focus on scalability and normalization."

Example Use:

Create a relational database schema for an online bookstore. Include tables for users, books, authors, orders, and reviews.

A.2 – CRUD API Generation

Prompt:

"Generate CRUD API endpoints for the [table/entity name] using best REST practices. Include method types, route names, and expected input/output."

Example Use:

Generate CRUD endpoints for a `product` table with fields: name, price, stock_quantity, and category_id.

A.3 – UI Component Generation

Prompt:

"Design frontend UI components for managing [entity name]. Include forms, input validation, and display tables using [framework]."

Example Use:

Design UI components for managing user accounts using React. Include a registration form, login form, and user list with edit/delete actions.

A.4 – Automation Workflow

Prompt:

"Create an automation workflow for [trigger] that performs [actions] and handles [exceptions]. Include step-by-step logic."

Example Use:

Create an automation workflow that sends a welcome email when a user signs up, logs the event, and retries email if it fails.

A.5 – Business Logic or Validation

Prompt:

"Add business logic to ensure [condition] before processing a [task]. Raise errors if [violation]."

Example Use:

Add business logic to ensure a product's stock_quantity is greater than 0 before placing an order. Raise a stock error if it isn't.

Prompt Template Summary Table

Task	Prompt Structure
Data Model Design	Create a relational schema for [use case]...
CRUD API	Generate API endpoints for [table/entity] with input/output formats...
UI Components	Design UI for [entity] using [framework] with validation and interaction...
Automation Workflow	Create a workflow for [trigger] to perform [actions] with fallback...

Business Rules / Validation	Add logic to ensure [rule] before proceeding with [task]...

Appendix B: Sample ERD and Schema Definitions

B.1 – ERD (Entity Relationship Diagram) – Text Format

Users

└── user_id (PK)

└── name

└── email

Products

└── product_id (PK)

└── name

└── category_id (FK)

└── stock_quantity

Categories

└── category_id (PK)

└── name

Orders

  └── order_id (PK)

  └── user_id (FK)

  └── order_date

Order_Items

  └── order_item_id (PK)

  └── order_id (FK)

  └── product_id (FK)

  └── quantity

B.2 – SQL Schema Definitions

```
CREATE TABLE users (

  user_id SERIAL PRIMARY KEY,

  name VARCHAR(100),

  email VARCHAR(100) UNIQUE

);


CREATE TABLE categories (
```

```
  category_id SERIAL PRIMARY KEY,

  name VARCHAR(100)

);


CREATE TABLE products (

  product_id SERIAL PRIMARY KEY,

  name VARCHAR(100),

  category_id INT REFERENCES categories(category_id),

  stock_quantity INT

);


CREATE TABLE orders (

  order_id SERIAL PRIMARY KEY,

  user_id INT REFERENCES users(user_id),

  order_date TIMESTAMP DEFAULT CURRENT_TIMESTAMP

);


CREATE TABLE order_items (

  order_item_id SERIAL PRIMARY KEY,

  order_id INT REFERENCES orders(order_id),

  product_id INT REFERENCES products(product_id),
```

```
quantity INT

);
```

Key Takeaways

- Use the ERD format to visualize data relationships with **indented lists and arrow references**.

- Keep SQL schema definitions clean and annotated for clarity.

- Prompt templates allow **reusability**, reducing cognitive load and maintaining consistency.

Appendix C: Debugging Cheat Sheet

Common Debugging Scenarios and Fixes

Problem Type	Symptoms	Solution
API not responding	404/500 errors, timeout	Check endpoint URL, method type, auth headers, or DeepAgent API definition

Database insert fails	SQL errors, validation errors	Validate schema types, required fields, and relationships
Form not updating data	No UI changes or stale data	Check data bindings, onChange handlers, and API response handling
Auth not working	Unauthorized errors	Confirm token flow, session storage, and user roles in business logic
Unexpected AI response	Wrong output, missing fields	Adjust prompt clarity, set stricter constraints, or provide examples in your prompt
UI component won't render	Blank area, console errors	Check component imports, rendering logic, and key props
Logic not triggering	No workflow execution	Inspect trigger conditions, ensure data events are firing properly
ORM not syncing	Model mismatch, migration errors	Verify ORM config, database migrations, and auto-sync status

Step-by-Step Debugging Checklist

1. **Start Small**: Test isolated components before full workflows.

2. **Use Console Logs**: Add temporary print/debug lines for logic paths.

3. **Validate Inputs**: Use sample payloads for API and DB testing.

4. **Check Dev Tools**: Inspect browser network tab for errors or dropped requests.

5. **Review DeepAgent Logs**: Use the platform's logs (if available) to review generated logic and triggers.

6. **Prompt Versioning**: Keep track of prompt changes to trace behavior regressions.

7. **Reset + Retry**: Regenerate the block or logic with tighter constraints if behavior remains inconsistent.

8. **Break Down Complex Prompts**: Split long instructions into steps or sub-prompts.

Best Practices

- **Add Assertions**: In testing, assert expected outcomes to catch silent failures.

- **Fallback Messages**: Include user-friendly error messages for better UI debugging.

- **Use Postman or curl**: Test APIs outside the app to isolate backend errors.

- **Code Reviews**: Use AI or peer review to verify business logic correctness.

Appendix D: Top 50 API Integrations to Try

Categories and Examples

Category	API Names
Communication	Twilio, SendGrid, Mailgun, Slack, Discord, WhatsApp Business API
Productivity Tools	Notion, Trello, Asana, ClickUp, Airtable, Google Calendar
CRM & Marketing	HubSpot, Salesforce, Pipedrive, Zoho CRM, ActiveCampaign
Payment Gateways	Stripe, PayPal, Razorpay, Square, Braintree
Cloud Storage	AWS S3, Google Drive, Dropbox, Box
E-commerce	Shopify, WooCommerce, Magento, BigCommerce
Analytics	Google Analytics, Mixpanel, Amplitude, Plausible

AI & NLP	OpenAI, Cohere, HuggingFace Inference, StabilityAI, Google PaLM
Social Media	Facebook Graph API, Twitter/X API, LinkedIn, Instagram Graph API
Customer Support	Intercom, Zendesk, Freshdesk, Crisp, HelpScout
DevOps/CI-CD	GitHub, GitLab, Bitbucket, Jenkins, CircleCI
Financial Services	Plaid, QuickBooks, Xero, Yodlee
Maps & Location	Google Maps, Mapbox, OpenStreetMap, HERE Maps
Forms & Surveys	Typeform, Google Forms API, JotForm, SurveyMonkey
OCR & Document Tools	Docparser, Nanonets, PDF.co, Tesseract OCR

Tips for Integration

- Use **built-in connectors** when available in DeepAgent for easy setup.

For unsupported APIs, use **custom REST integration prompts**:

Prompt Example:

Connect to the Stripe API using a secret key. Retrieve the list of customers and display them in a UI table.

-
- Secure all APIs with proper **authentication (OAuth2, API keys)**.

- Handle **rate limits** and **errors gracefully** with retry logic.

Integration Best Practices

- **Test in Isolation First**: Validate API manually before embedding in flows.

- **Document Keys and Endpoints**: Maintain a config file or .env for easy portability.

- **Limit Scope**: Use only the API features you need to avoid over-engineering.

- **Set Timeouts and Alerts**: Ensure no infinite waits or silent failures.

- **Use Caching**: For frequently accessed data like analytics or CRM leads.

Appendix E: Further Reading and Resources

Explore these curated resources to deepen your understanding of AI agents, LLMs, app development, and automation workflows:

Books

Title	Author(s)	Description
Architecting the Cloud	Michael J. Kavis	Modern cloud application design principles.
Designing Data-Intensive Applications	Martin Kleppmann	Deep dive into data systems and their trade-offs.
Building Intelligent Systems	Geoff Hulten	Real-world guidance on production-ready AI systems.
Human Compatible	Stuart Russell	Explores alignment and safety in AI development.

AI & LLM Resources

Resource	Type	Description
OpenAI API Documentation	Docs	Comprehensive guide to using OpenAI APIs.
LangChain Documentation	Docs	Build apps powered by LLMs with chains and agents.
AutoGen by Microsoft	Docs/Repo	Framework for multi-agent workflows and orchestration.

Automation Tools and Guides

Tool/Platform	Link	Description
n8n	https://n8n.io	Open-source workflow automation.
Zapier	https://zapier.com	No-code automation across SaaS tools.
Pipedream	https://pipedream.com	Low-code workflows with APIs and events.

YouTube & Video Playlists

Channel/Creator	Focus Area
Fireship	Modern dev and AI concepts in short videos.
OpenAI	Official updates and tutorials.
ThePrimeagen	Practical coding and app-building series.

Communities and Forums

Community	Link
Dev.to	https://dev.to
r/ArtificialIntelligence	https://reddit.com/r/artificial
Indie Hackers	https://indiehackers.com
DeepAgent Discord	(Include invite link if public)

Glossary

A

- **AGI (Artificial General Intelligence)**: A type of AI that can perform any intellectual task that a human can. It contrasts with narrow AI, which is designed for specific tasks.

- **API (Application Programming Interface)**: A set of protocols and tools that allow different software applications to communicate with each other.

- **API Key**: A unique identifier used to authenticate a user or system to access an API.

- **Automation Workflow**: A series of steps or tasks that are automatically executed based on specific triggers, often with minimal or no human intervention.

B

- **Backend**: The server-side part of an application responsible for database interactions, user authentication, and business logic. It typically runs behind the scenes.

- **BPM (Business Process Management)**: A systematic approach to improving and automating the processes within an organization, often using workflows and AI agents.

C

- **CRUD (Create, Read, Update, Delete)**: The four basic operations used to manage data in a database.

- **Chatbot**: A software application designed to simulate human conversation, often powered by AI and integrated into applications for customer service or user interaction.

- **Continuous Integration (CI)**: A software development practice in which code changes are automatically tested and integrated into a shared repository.

D

- **DeepAgent**: A no-code AI development platform that allows users to create, configure, and deploy intelligent applications powered by machine learning models, APIs, and automation workflows.

- **Database Schema**: A blueprint or structure that defines the organization of data in a database, including tables, columns, data types, and relationships.

- **Deployment**: The process of making an application accessible for use by users, often by hosting it on servers or cloud platforms.

E

- **Entity Relationship Diagram (ERD)**: A visual representation of the entities within a system and the relationships between them, typically used to design databases.

- **End-to-End Testing**: Testing the entire application workflow from start to finish to ensure everything functions as expected.

F

- **Frontend**: The client-side part of an application, responsible for the user interface (UI) and interaction with the user.

- **Fine-Tuning**: The process of adjusting and optimizing machine learning models to better perform specific tasks based on user input and feedback.

G

- **GraphQL**: A query language for APIs and a runtime for executing those queries by using a type system that defines the data.

- **GitHub Actions**: An automation platform that enables continuous integration and continuous delivery (CI/CD) workflows in GitHub repositories.

H

- **Hosting**: The process of storing and maintaining a website or application on a server to make it accessible over the internet.

- **HTTP (Hypertext Transfer Protocol)**: A protocol used for transferring web pages and data over the internet, crucial for APIs and web applications.

I

- **Integration**: The process of connecting different software systems or services to work together seamlessly.

- **Intelligent Decision Making**: The use of AI agents and algorithms to make autonomous or semi-autonomous decisions based on data.

J

- **Jira**: A popular project management tool used for tracking tasks, bugs, and agile workflows, often integrated with other tools via APIs.

L

- **LLM (Large Language Model)**: A type of AI model designed to process and generate human language. LLMs, such as GPT, can assist with tasks like text generation, summarization, and code completion.

- **LLM API**: An API that allows users to access and integrate language models like GPT for tasks such as natural language processing and conversational agents.

M

- **Machine Learning (ML)**: A subset of AI focused on developing algorithms that allow systems to learn from data and improve over time.

- **Model Fine-Tuning**: The process of refining a pre-trained AI model with additional data or specific tasks to make it more accurate for a given application.

N

- **NoSQL Database**: A type of database that does not use the traditional relational model, designed for scalable, flexible storage of unstructured data (e.g., MongoDB, Cassandra).

- **Normalization**: The process of organizing a relational database to reduce redundancy and dependency by dividing large tables into smaller, manageable ones.

P

- **Prompt Engineering**: The practice of designing and refining input queries to generate optimal outputs from AI models like LLMs.

- **Public API**: An API made available for use by the public, often with documentation and access protocols.

R

- **REST API**: A type of web service that follows REST (Representational State Transfer) principles, commonly used to create scalable and stateless APIs.

- **Rate Limiting**: A technique used to control the amount of incoming traffic to an API, often to prevent abuse or overuse of resources.

S

- **Serverless Architecture**: A cloud computing model where the cloud provider automatically manages the infrastructure, allowing developers to focus on code and applications without worrying about servers.

- **Schema Definition**: The structure of a database, including tables, columns, relationships, and constraints.

T

- **Tokenization**: In natural language processing, the process of breaking down text into smaller units, such as words or sentences.

- **Testing and Debugging**: The process of running software to identify bugs and issues, and then resolving them.

U

- **UI (User Interface)**: The visual elements of an application with which users interact.

- **User Authentication**: The process of verifying the identity of a user before granting access to an application or system.

W

- **Webhooks**: HTTP callbacks used to send real-time data from one system to another, often used in automation workflows.

- **Workflow Automation**: The design and execution of predefined sequences of tasks triggered by specific conditions or events.

Index

L

- LLM (Large Language Model)

- LLM APIs

M

- Model Customization

- Machine Learning (ML)

- Multi-Agent Collaboration

N

- NoSQL

- Normalization

O

- OAuth2

- Optimizing AI Prompts

P

- Prompt Engineering

- Privacy Compliance

U

- UI (User Interface)

- User Authentication

- Unit Testing

V

- Vercel Deployment

W

- Webhooks

- Workflow Automation

- Working with Databases

Z

- Zero-Code Setup